The Complete
Beginning Guitarist

A fun, creative, and comprehensive method for new musicians

Aaron Stang
Bill Purse

Guitar photos courtesy of Taylor Guitars and Paul Reed Smith Guitars.

Alfred

Alfred Publishing Co., Inc.
16320 Roscoe Blvd., Suite 100
P.O. Box 10003
Van Nuys, CA 91410-0003
alfred.com

ISBN-10: 0-7390-5143-1 (Book & 2 CDs)
ISBN-13: 978-0-7390-5143-6 (Book & 2 CDs)

MW00386570

CONTENTS	PAGE	CD 1

 For free downloadable MP3 files for all the CD tracks, and free interactive software versions of selected tracks, go to alfred.com/expressions/cbg.htm.

CONTENTS	PAGE	CD 2

CONTENTS	PAGE	CD 2

The modern guitar, in its current form—six strings and a standardized tuning—is less than 200 years old. However, guitar-like instruments have been popular in every culture and region of the world for a millennium or more. The guitar and its predecessors have been primarily folk instruments—developed by local cultures and used in the performance of local, indigenous music. These instruments have been relatively easy to build and play and were perfect for creating simple instrumental accompaniments for singers and dancers. And due to the innate emotive nature of these stringed instruments—their ability to create subtle emotional shadings and nuance—they remain one of the most popular instruments in the world in all styles and genres.

In this course you will play melodies and chords on the guitar. You will create your own guitar accompaniments and perform solos, duets, and ensembles. You will explore the basic principles of music—known as music theory—and how it relates to the guitar so that on your own you can explore and experience guitar music of any style you choose. Plus, you will perform in a wide variety musical styles as you learn about the cultures and environments from which those styles developed and how the guitar finds its niche in all of them.

The guitar is a unique instrument that allows performers to shape it to their own personalities and musical interests. It can be used by a singer/songwriter to create simple yet beautiful song accompaniments, or it can be wielded by a rock guitar virtuoso to create thundering lead solos that leave an audience in awe. The guitar finds its way to the world's concert stages in concerto performances by classical guitar masters with full orchestra accompaniment, and in the hands of a blues master it can sing and cry. Our hope is that this book will help you find your voice on this wonderful and personal instrument.

The Authors,

Aaron Stang   Bill Purse

NEW CONTENT

NEW VOCABULARY

bar line: A line that divides the staff into measures

ledger line: A short line placed above or below a staff to extend the lines and spaces

measure: The space between two bar lines to form a grouping of beats

staff: Five lines and four spaces on which notes and other musical symbols are placed

time signature: The symbol at the beginning of the staff that indicates the meter. The upper number indicates the number of beats in each measure, and the lower number indicates which kind of note receives the beat.

treble clef: The staff on which notes are above middle C

Acoustic Guitar

Electric Guitar

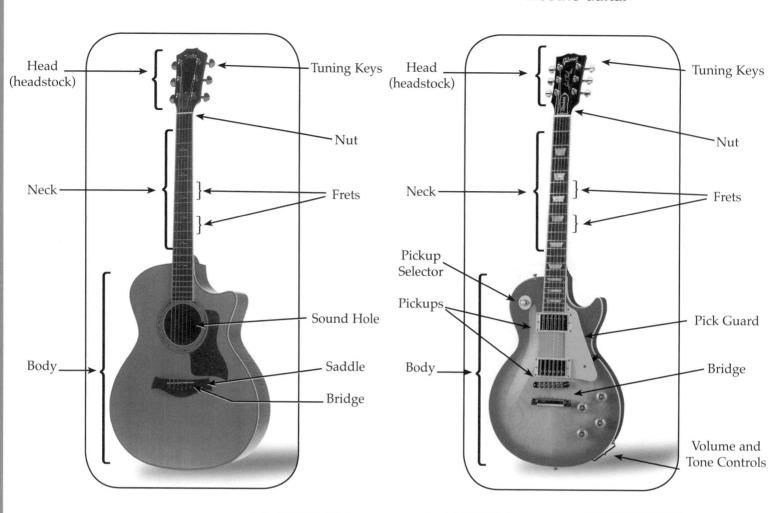

Head (headstock)

Tuning Keys

Nut

Neck

Frets

Body

Sound Hole

Saddle

Bridge

Head (headstock)

Tuning Keys

Nut

Neck

Frets

Pickup Selector

Pickups

Pick Guard

Body

Bridge

Volume and Tone Controls

Guitar headstocks generally fall into two categories:

Three on a Side

Six in Line

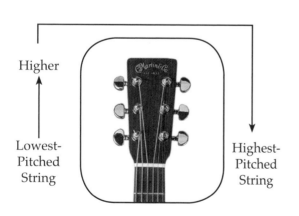

Higher

Lowest-Pitched String

Highest-Pitched String

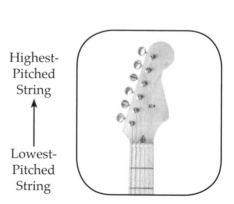

Highest-Pitched String

Lowest-Pitched String

Steel-String Acoustic

The steel-string acoustic guitar is probably the most common guitar type and one of the most versatile. It is a perfect accompaniment instrument and works well played with a pick or with the fingers. It is also very appropriate for solo guitar music. The steel-string acoustic guitar can be used to perform virtually any style of music.

Nylon-String Acoustic

The nylon-string acoustic guitar has a softer, mellower sound than the steel-string. Nylon-string guitars are often played finger-style and are closely associated with Spanish, classical, and Latin American styles of guitar music.

Electric Guitar

The electric guitar is also versatile but is most often associated with rock, blues, country, and jazz music. The electric guitar works extremely well in a band situation and is usually played with a pick.

Sitting Position (with strap)

Sitting Position (no strap)

Classical Position

Standing Position

Right Arm

Rest your right elbow on top of the guitar as shown in the photos above. Do not hang your arm in front of the guitar where it would interfere with the vibration of the guitar's top.

Left Arm: The Neck Wrap

Wrap your left hand completely around the top of the guitar neck, as in the photo on the right. This natural grasp aligns the knuckles with the strings, which is necessary for good guitar technique. Now roll your left hand toward the floor, sliding your arched fingertips down to the first string (nearest the floor), with your thumb remaining centered behind the neck. By keeping your knuckles aligned with the strings, especially while playing chords, you will get the best sound with the least amount of effort.

The Pick

Guitar picks are made of plastic and come in a variety of shapes, sizes, and thickness: thin, medium, and heavy. The traditional tear-drop shaped guitar pick in a medium thickness is a good choice for a beginning guitarist. Heavy picks are often preferred by electric lead guitarists, and light picks can sound especially appealing when used to strum an acoustic guitar.

When using the pick, there are two distinct directions: down (toward the floor) and up (toward the ceiling). It's best to realize that the up movement is really just the result of returning your hand to its starting position—so when done properly, a down-up strum is one continuous, fluid movement, not two (separate) ones.

The down-strokes and up-strokes of the pick are represented with the following symbols. These same symbols also indicate the bow direction for string players.

Down-stroke: ⊓   Up-stroke: V

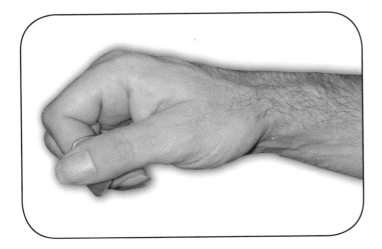

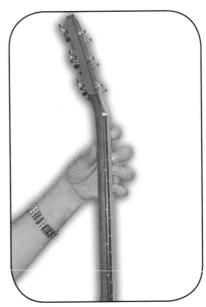

The pick should be held between the thumb and the index finger. Don't grip it tightly. The pick should be held just firm enough so that you don't drop it but lightly enough so that someone could easily remove it from your grasp. The elbow of your picking arm acts as a pivot to help you move the pick from string to string.

The thumb should be placed behind the neck, approximately behind your second finger. The fingers should be placed directly behind the frets, not on top of them or centered between them.

Strumming and Picking Exercises

- **Exercise 1:** Beginning with the 6th string (the thickest one), pick each string. Use the weight of your hand and forearm to drop your pick through (try not to push it through) the string and allow it to come to rest on the next string. Then play the next string, and so on.

- **Exercise 2:** Now strum all six strings: Hold your pick loosely and let your hand glide rapidly through all six strings. Strive for one sound, not six separate attacks.

- **Exercise 3:** Try using alternating down-strokes and up-strokes to play the 1st string. Hold the pick loosely so that there is no resistance to the pick in either direction.

The Importance of Warming Up

Playing the guitar is an athletic workout for the wrist and fingers. Just as a smart runner stretches and warms up before training for a big race, a smart guitarist stretches his or her finger and hand muscles before practicing or playing a big concert.

1) Gentle Finger Pull-Back and Tug

Gently pull back and stretch your hands.

Gently tug and stretch your hands.

2) Wrist Rotation

Touch the tip of your thumb to the tip of the other three fingers with the left and your elbows at your sides, rotate your several times like airplane propellers.

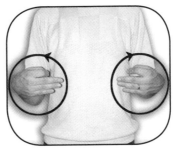

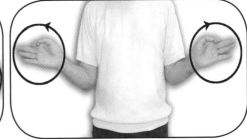

3) 1, 2, 3 Between-the-Finger Stretch

Place your right-hand index finger between the index and middle finger of your left hand and gently massage the base of the fingers. Then add your right-hand middle finger and repeat, and finally the ring finger. Move to the next pair of left-hand fingers.

To play chords cleanly, it is important that the nails of the left hand are kept short to allow the tips of the fingers to depress the strings. A proper length will allow your fingertips and nails to make contact with a flat surface, such as a table, at the same time.

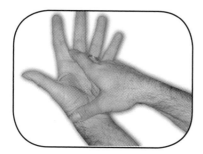  

Tuning the Guitar

Following are several methods for tuning your guitar. No matter what tuning method you use, here are a few basic tips:

- It is always easier to tune up to the correct pitch than to tune the string down. This is because our ears seem to hear when a note is flat (below pitch) more clearly than when a note is sharp (above the correct pitch). So begin by making sure that your guitar string sounds lower than the correct pitch. If the string sounds sharp, loosen it until you know for sure that it has gone below the tuning note, and then begin to tighten it slowly, bringing it up to pitch.

- When tuning a guitar in the classroom or any noisy environment, move your ear closer to the guitar to hear your instrument more clearly.

Tuning Your Guitar to the Included CD

Your teacher has a CD with a tuning track. Beginning with your 1st string (closest to the floor), turn the correct tuning key until your string comes up to match the pitch on the CD. If necessary, bring the string flat first so that you can then tune up to the correct pitch.

Electronic Tuners

Many brands of small battery-operated tuners, similar to the one shown in Figure 1, are available. Simply follow the instructions supplied with your tuner.

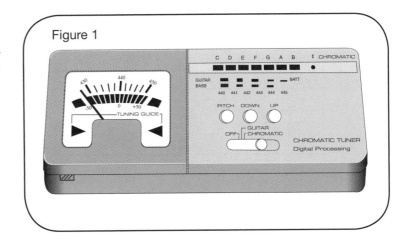

Figure 1

Tuning the Guitar to a Piano

One of the easiest ways to tune a guitar is to a piano keyboard. The six strings of the guitar are tuned to the keyboard notes, as shown in Figure 2.

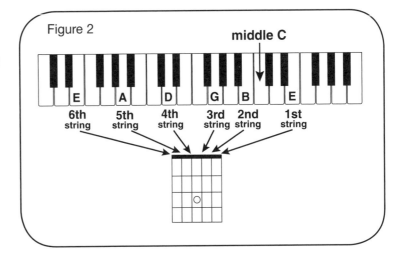

Figure 2

middle C

E   A   D   G   B   E
6th   5th   4th   3rd 2nd   1st
string   string   string   string string string

Tuning the Guitar to Itself (Relative Tuning)

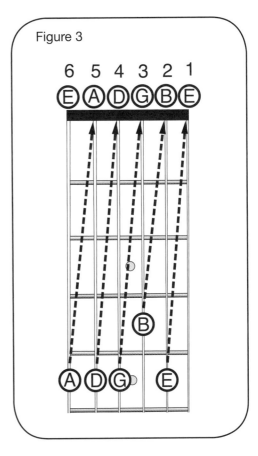

Figure 3

1. Tune the 6th string to E on the piano (or some other fixed-pitch instrument). You can also use a pitch pipe or an electronic guitar tuner.

2. Depress the 6th string at the 5th fret. Play it and you will hear the note A, which is the same note as the 5th string open. Turn the 5th-string tuning key until the pitch of the 5th string matches that of the 6th string.

3. Depress the 5th string at the 5th fret. Play it and you will hear the note D, which is the same note as the 4th string open. Turn the 4th-string tuning key until the pitch of the 4th string matches that of the 5th string.

4. Depress the 4th string at the 5th fret. Play it and you will hear the note G, which is the same note as the 3rd string open. Turn the 3rd-string tuning key until the pitch of the 3rd string matches that of the 4th string.

5. Depress the 3rd string at the 4th fret. Play it and you will hear the note B, which is the same note as the 2nd string open. Turn the 2nd-string tuning key until the pitch of the 2nd string matches that of the 3rd string.

6. Depress the 2nd string at the 5th fret. Play it and you will hear the note E, which is the same note as the 1st string open. Turn the 1st-string tuning key until the pitch of the 1st string matches that of the 2nd string.

There are seven natural notes. They are named for the first seven letters of the alphabet: A B C D E F G. After G, we begin again with A. Music is written on a **staff.** The staff consists of five lines with four spaces between the lines.

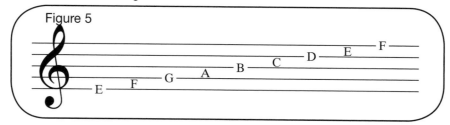
Figure 4

At the beginning of the staff is a treble or G clef. (The treble clef is known as the G clef because it encircles the 2nd line G.) The clef determines the location of notes on the staff. All guitar music is written on a **treble clef.**

The notes are written on the staff in alphabetical order. The first line is E.

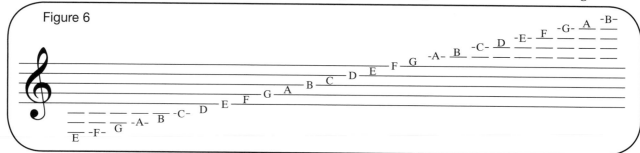
Figure 5

Notes can extend above and below the treble clef. When they do, **ledger lines** are added. Following is the approximate range of the guitar from the lowest note, open 6th string E, to B on the first string, 17th fret.

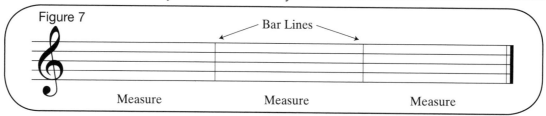
Figure 6

The staff is divided into **measures** by **bar lines.** A heavy double bar line marks the end of the music.

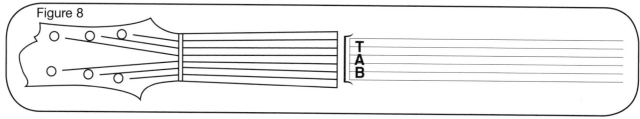
Figure 7

Tablature is a type of music notation that is specific to the guitar; its use dates back to the 1600s. Tablature (also known as "tab") illustrates the location of notes on the neck of the guitar. Tab is usually used in conjunction with a music staff. The notes and rhythms are indicated in the music staff; the tab shows where those notes are played on the guitar.

Figure 8

The location of any note is indicated by the placement of fret numbers on the strings.

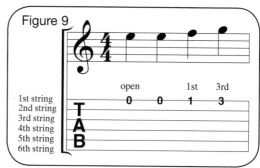
Figure 9

At the beginning of every song is a **time signature.** 4/4 is the most common time signature:

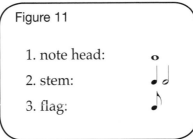

Figure 10

4/4 four counts to a measure
a quarter note receives one count

The top number tells you how many counts per measure.

The bottom number tells you which kind of note receives one count.

The time value of a note is determined by three things:

Figure 11

1. note head: o

2. stem:

3. flag:

o This is a whole note. The note head is open and has no stem. In 4/4 time, a whole note receives four counts.

This is a half note. It has an open note head and a stem. A half note receives two counts.

This is a quarter note. It has a solid note head and a stem. A quarter note receives one count.

This is an eighth note. It has a solid note head and a stem with a flag attached. An eighth note receives a half count.

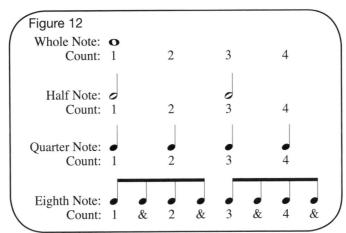

Figure 12

Whole Note: o			
Count: 1	2	3	4

Half Note:			
Count: 1	2	3	4

Quarter Note:			
Count: 1	2	3	4

Eighth Note:							
Count: 1	&	2	&	3	&	4	&

Count aloud and clap the rhythm to this excerpt from "Jingle Bells." **CD 1:5**

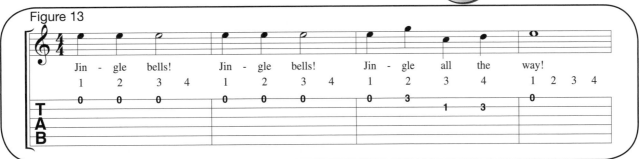

Figure 13

Jin	-	gle	bells!	Jin	-	gle	bells!	Jin	-	gle	all	the	way!
1		2	3	4	1		2	3	4	1		2	3	4	1	2	3	4

4/4 conducting pattern:

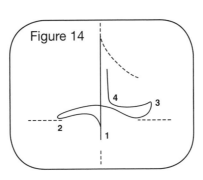

Figure 14

Flamenco Guitar

Flamenco is the native folk music of the Andalusian Gypsies from southern Spain.
Flamenco is not just a musical style—but an art form combining music, song and dance.

NEW CONTENT

Melodic
    New Notes on the 1st String:
      E, F, and G
    Rhythms: Quarter Note, Half Note,
      Whole Note
    Time Signature: 4/4
    Ear Training
    Songs:
      "Folk Song"
      "The Blues Beat"

Stylistic
    About Flamenco Music
    Artist Portrait: Paco de Lucía
    Time Signature: 3/4
    Song: "Flamenco Fantasy"

Chordal
    C and G7
    Strum Pattern 1
    Creating/Improvising New
      Strum Patterns

Theory
    Key of C, C Scale
    The C and G7 Chords
    I and **V7** Chords
    Theory Worksheet
    Improvise Accompaniment to
      "He's Got the Whole World
      in His Hands"
    Two-Chord Song List

NEW VOCABULARY

quarter note (♩):	Receives one count
half note (♪):	Receives two counts
dotted half note (♩.):	Receives three counts
whole note (o):	Receives four counts
time signature:	**4** = Four counts to a measure **4** = A quarter note receives one count
down-stroke (⊓):	Push the pick through the string with a downward attack (toward the floor)
chord:	Three or more tones sounded at the same time
tonic:	The **I** chord
dominant:	The **V** chord
flamenco (*flah-MEHN-koh*):	Style of music from Andalusia in Spain
Andalusia (*an-duh-LOO-zhuh*) (Spanish: Andalucía [*ahn-dah-loo-SEE-ah*]):	Region of southern Spain where flamenco was born and developed
tarantas (*tahr-AHN-tahs*):	A rhythmically free-form style used to accompany singers
soleares (*soh-leh-AH-rehs*):	The mother of flamenco song; consists of 12 beats, usually played slowly, with accents on beats 3, 6, 8, 10, and 12.
alegrías (*ah-leh-GREE-ahs*):	A joyful dance, from the traditional folk music of Aragón
rumba (*ROOM-bah*):	Lively style typified by many pop-flamenco artists such as Gipsy Kings; characterized by rapid syncopated strumming with the whole right hand.
rasgueado (*RAHS-geh-ah-doh*):	Rapid strumming technique unique to flamenco guitarists
golpe (*GOHL-peh*):	Percussive beats tapped by the guitarist on the top of the guitar, to create the appropriate accents

New Notes: E, F, and G

(See page 12 for a complete overview of music notation and tablature.)

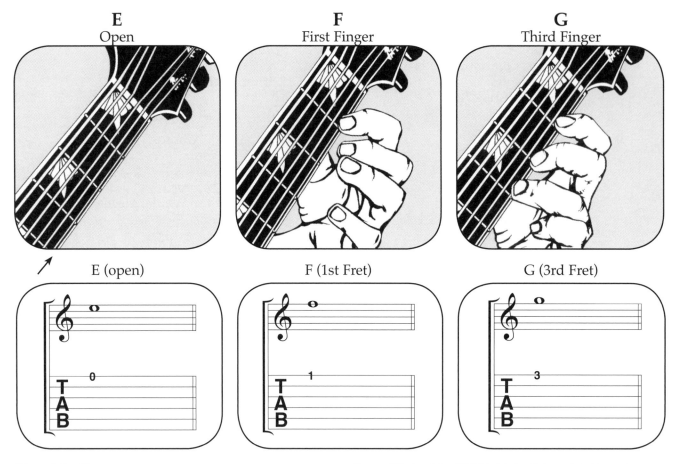

New Rhythms

(See page 13 for a complete overview of rhythm notation.)

Quarter note: ♩ = one count

Half note: ♩ = two counts

Whole note: 𝅝 = four counts

Time Signature

4 = Four counts to a measure

4 = A quarter note receives one count

Songs in **4/4** receive four counts per measure.

Music Examples: Play all notes with a down-stroke of the pick (⊓). Strike the string with a downward attack (toward the floor). CD 1:7

Example 1: Quarter Notes

Example 2: Half Notes

Example 3: Whole Notes

SECTION 2 • The Notes on the 1st String

Ear Training: Your teacher will play a C chord and give you a starting pitch.

Example 1: Sing: Do, Re, Mi, Fa, Sol (C, D, E, F, G)

Sing:

Do Re Mi Fa Sol   Do Re Mi Fa Sol

Example 2: Sing and then play: Mi, Fa, Sol (E, F, G)

Sing: Play: Sing: Play:

Mi Fa Sol   E F G   Mi Fa Sol   E F G

Example 3: Sing and then play: Sol, Mi, Fa (G, F, E)

Sing: Play: Sing: Play:

Sol Fa Mi   G F E   Sol Fa Mi   G F E

Folk Song

Note Throughout the book, gray chord symbols above the notes are for teacher accompaniment. They are not note names.

TIP Always count wiwth a steady beat—like the ticking of a clock. Don't slow down, speed up, or pause.

The Blues Beat

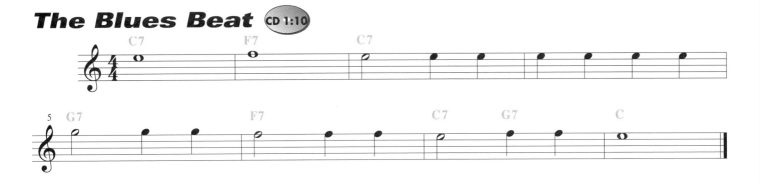

About Flamenco Music

Flamenco music is closely associated with a region of Spain known as Andalusia. In fact, flamenco is the native folk music of the Andalusia Gypsies from southern Spain. Flamenco is not only a musical style but also an art form combining music, song, and dance. Flamenco musicians often grow up totally immersed in the culture of flamenco music. Many of the greatest flamenco artists are born into families that have been performing, dancing, and singing flamenco music for several generations. Some of the greats include Ramón Montoya, Sabicas, and Paco de Lucía. CD Track 11 is an example of the flamenco guitar style.

Most flamenco music is based on specific dances and vocal forms. Each dance is accompanied by a very specific rhythmic pattern called "the compass," and each of the dance forms is usually associated with a specific mode (scale) and key center. Each form has a mood, or feelingly, associated with it (sad, happy, etc.). Some flamenco forms, such as the **tarantas,** are based on accompanying a vocalist and are played very freely. Within these pre-determined forms the musicians are free to improvise. Flamenco music is improvised and the forms are passed down from generation to generation; the music is not usually notated. However, the improvisations must always support the dancers or singers. Some of the most common of these dance forms are the **soleares*,** the **alegrías,** and the **rumba.** Listen to CD Track 12 for a sample of each. Describe the different mood that each form evokes.

Flamenco guitarists use several highly specialized guitar techniques. Some of the most easily identifiable are the **rasgueado**—the guitarist rapidly fans his right-hand fingers across the strings, creating a very rhythmic strumming effect—and the **golpe**—the guitarist taps on the top of his guitar to create percussive, drum-like accents. Listen to CD Track 12 and identify these two techniques.

About Flamenco Guitars

The flamenco guitar is a Spanish instrument similar to the classical guitar. Like the classical guitar, it has nylon strings. The strings on a flamenco guitar are usually very close to the fingerboard, making it easier to play the lightning-quick runs associated with this style. Flamenco guitars are made of cypress and spruce, giving them a much brighter sound than classical guitars. The guitars usually have violin-style tuning keys instead of modern tuners with metal gears, and they have plastic tap plates on the top. Flamenco guitarists often use their fingernails to tap out rhythms and loud accents on these tap plates. Without the tap plate, a guitarist would quickly wear holes right through the top of the instrument. Also, a capo, or *cejilla,* is used to transpose keys to conform to the singer's voice. The capo adds to the brightness and ease of playing for the guitarist.

*CD Track 14 is a demonstration of the soleares.

Artist Portrait: Paco de Lucía

Paco de Lucía, like many of the great flamenco artists, is from a family of flamenco performers; his father, brothers, and sister all perform as guitarists, dancers, and singers. Paco's constant experimentation and stunning virtuoso technique have revolutionized flamenco music and brought the flamenco guitar from its traditional role as an accompaniment instrument for dancers and singers to its current status as a featured instrument on the world's concert stages.

New Time Signature: $\frac{3}{4}$ $\frac{3}{4}$ conducting pattern:

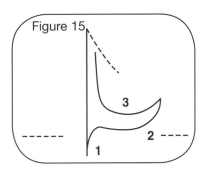

$\frac{3}{4}$ = Three counts to a measure

$\frac{3}{4}$ = A quarter note receives one count

Songs in $\frac{3}{4}$ receive three counts per measure.

A dotted half note receives three counts: 𝅗𝅥. = three counts

Flamenco Fantasy CD 1:13

About Chords

- A **chord** consists of three or more notes played at the same time.

- **Chord symbols** indicate the name of a chord:

    Major chords are indicated simply by the letter name of the chord (also called the root). For example: "C" would indicate a C major chord.

    Minor chords are indicated by the letter name and a lowercase "m" indicating minor. For example: C minor is "Cm."

    Dominant 7th chords are indicated by the letter name of the chord plus the number 7. For example: G dominant 7 is "G7."

Note: Major, minor, and dominant 7th are the three basic chord families. All chords fit into one of these three families. As you play them, you will see that each chord type (major, minor, and dominant 7th) has a very different type of sound than the others.

Ear Training: CD Tracks 15 and 17 contain explanations and demonstrations of these chords. CD Tracks 16 and 18 contain examples for you to identify. Listen for the differences in each chord type. Try to identify them "by ear." Describe them.

Chord fingerings are illustrated with **chord frame diagrams,** as shown in Figure 16.

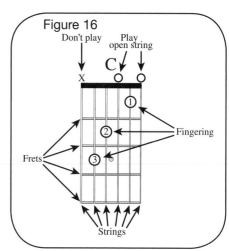

The C and G7 Chords

To play the C chord:

- Place your third finger on the 5th string, just behind the 3rd fret.

- Place your second finger on the 4th string, just behind the 2nd fret.

- Place your first finger on the 2nd string, just behind the 1st fret.

- Don't play the 6th string. The 3rd and 1st strings are played open.

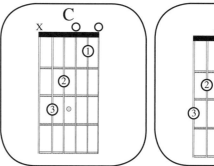

To play the G7 chord:

- Place your third finger on the 6th string, just behind the 3rd fret.

- Place your second finger on the 5th string, just behind the 2nd fret.

- Place your first finger on the 1st string, just behind the 1st fret.

- The 4th, 3rd, and 2nd strings are played open.

Practice each chord. Strum through the chord and try to get a clear sound with all the notes ringing.

Notice how similar the two chord shapes are: To change from C to G7, just spread out your fingering—all three fingers should move simultaneously, not one at a time: Your first finger shifts from the 2nd string to the 1st string, while your second and third fingers shift from the 4th and 5th strings to the 5th and 6th strings.

Strum-and-Sing Style The guitar is a perfect instrument for accompanying yourself or another singer. In fact, the style of strum-and-sing guitar is so popular and important that many famous singer/songwriters use the guitar only for accompaniment, not as a melodic or lead instrument. One of the nice things about strum-and-sing style is that, armed with 15 or 16 important chords and some imagination, you can make a boundless amount of music.

This next example combines the C and G7 chords. The **rhythm slashes** indicate that you should strum the complete chord with the indicated rhythm (steady quarter notes). The last strum is a half note.

Strum Pattern 1 CD 1:20

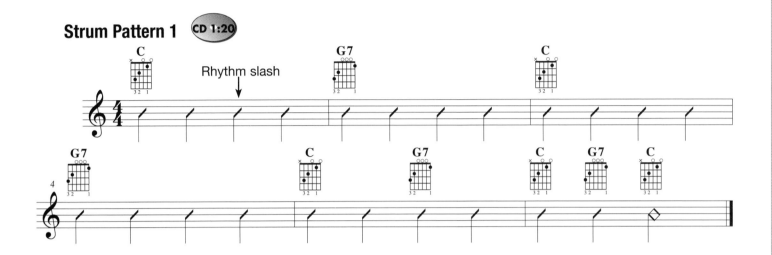

 It is helpful to develop mental snapshots of chord fingerings so that you can easily recall the fingerings.

Create Your Own Strum Rhythm CD 1:21

Often, guitarists **improvise** the rhythm pattern of their strum as they play. In this next chord progression try to make up your own strum patterns. Use just whole-note, half-note, and quarter-note rhythms. Follow the chord progression and tap your foot. Keep a steady four beats per measure.

Strum marks (the four slash marks in each measure) indicate that you should improvise your own strum pattern.

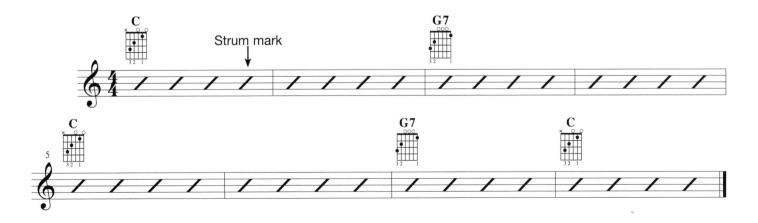

Here is a C major scale: C   D   E   F   G   A   B   C

Play a C chord. Listen to the chord and sing the C scale: Do Re Mi Fa Sol La Ti Do

The C chord (C-E-G) is built on the **first** note of the scale.
The G7 chord (G-B-D-F) is built on the **fifth** note of the scale.

C	D	E	F	G	A	B	C
1	2	3	4	5	6	7	8

Play a C chord. Listen to the chord and sing the root (C) and the 5th (G): Do Sol Do

Theory Worksheet

Chords are identified (labeled) with Roman numerals. So, in the key of C, the C chord is the **I** chord (pronounced *one* chord) and the G chord is the **V** chord (*five* chord). Since G is the **V** chord, G7 is the **V7** chord (*five-seven* chord).

C	D	E	F	G	A	B	C
I				V			

Following are the G, D, A, and E major scales. Fill in the blanks.

G major:

G   A   B   C   D   E   F#   G

What is the **I** chord? _____

What is the **V7** chord? _____

D major:

D   E   F#   G   A   B   C#   D

What is the **I** chord? _____

What is the **V7** chord? _____

A major:

A   B   C#   D   E   F#   G#   A

What is the **I** chord? _____

What is the **V7** chord? _____

E major:

E   F#   G#   A   B   C#   D#   E

What is the **I** chord? _____

What is the **V7** chord? _____

The **V** chord can be a simple major chord (a G chord in the key of C) or it can be a dominant 7th (G7 in the key of C). The **V7** tends to want to resolve back to the **I** chord stronger than the plain **V** chord does.

 Musicians call the **I** chord the **tonic** and the **V** chord the **dominant**.

Improvising and Ear Training

"He's Got the Whole World in His Hands" uses just two chords: the **I** and the **V7** (C and G7). In the arrangement below, only the lyrics, not the chords, are indicated. Try one of the following:

- Sing the song to yourself, begin on the C chord, strum along, and use your ear to determine when to change from the C to the G7 and back again (when the chord clashes with the melody).

- The song is sung on the CD. Listen to it with the guitar accompaniment, then turn your stereo balance to the left (minus guitar), and let your ear guide you as to when to change from the C to the G7 and back again.

He's Got the Whole World in His Hands

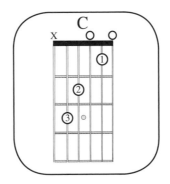 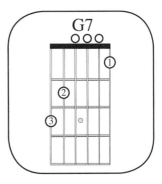

Verses 1 and 3:

He's got the whole world in his hands,

He's got the whole world in his hands,

He's got the whole world in his hands,

He's got the whole world in his hands.

Verse 2:

He's got itty-bitty baby in his hands,

He's got itty-bitty baby in his hands,

He's got itty-bitty baby in his hands,

He's got itty-bitty baby in his hands.

Following is a list of songs that use only the **I** and **V7** chords. Pick a song you know and try to sing the melody while accompanying yourself on the guitar. Make up your own strum pattern and use your ear to figure out when to change chords.

Two-Chord Songs

"Down in the Valley"

"My Darlin' Clementine"

"Farmer in the Dell"

"Mary Had a Little Lamb"

"Merrily We Roll Along"

"Polly Wolly Doodle"

"Shoo Fly Don't Bother Me"

"Three Blind Mice"

"Yellow Submarine" (the chorus)

Folk Guitar

Folk music in America is often associated with "protest" music because many of the early folk songs protested harsh working conditions, war, and other social issues.

NEW CONTENT

Melodic
New Notes on the 2nd String:
  B, C, and D
Ear Training
New Concepts: Ties, Quarter Rest
Songs:
  "Flamenco Fantasy" (Duet)
  "The Blues Beat"
  "Jingle Bells"
  "When the Saints Go Marching In"

Stylistic
About Folk Music
"Folk Song" (Duet)
Chordal
Eighth Notes
Down-Strokes and Up-Strokes
The Down-Up Strum
Strum Patterns 2 and 3
Songs:
  "Folk Song" (Ensemble)
  "Strum Pattern 3" (Bass Note/Strum)
  "Jambalaya"
Artist Portrait: Hank Williams

NEW VOCABULARY

duet:	A piece of music with two interacting parts
tie:	A curved line connecting two notes of the same pitch and played as if they were one
rest:	The symbol for a silent unit of time
eighth notes:	Half the length of a quarter note. Two eighth notes equal a quarter note.
up-stroke (∨):	Drag the pick back up through the string (toward the ceiling). Usually the up-stroke immediately follows a down-stroke, returning your hand to its original position.
folk music:	The indigenous (local) music that develops within a specific region or culture
harmony:	Two or more musical tones sounding at the same time

The Notes on the 2nd String

New Notes: B, C, and D

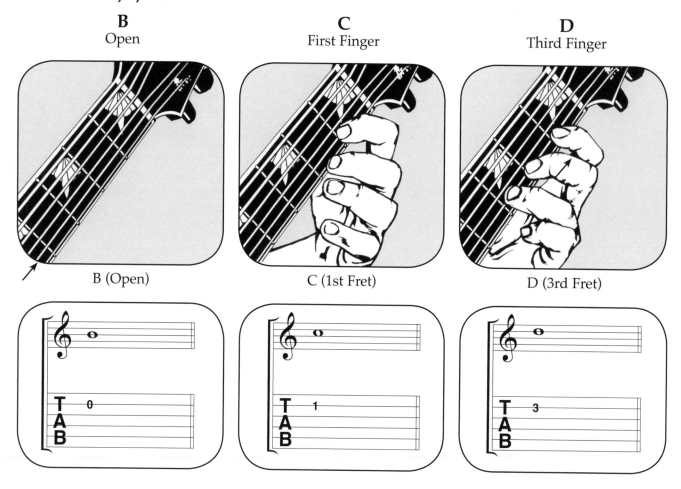

Example 1

Example 2: Notes on the 1st and 2nd Strings

Ear Training

Example 1: Play a C chord. Sing and then play: Do, Re, Do, Ti, Do (C, D, C, B, C)

Example 2: Sing and then play: Do, Re, Mi, Fa, Sol (C, D, E, F, G)

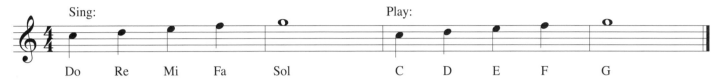

Example 3: Sing and then play: Sol, Fa, Mi, Re, Do, Ti, Do (G, F, E, D, C, B, C)

Following is a second guitar part for "Flamenco Fantasy" (see page 19). All of the notes for this second guitar part are on the 2nd string. Once you've learned this song, it should be played as a duet with the first guitar part from page 19.

Flamenco Fantasy (Duet Part) CD 1:25

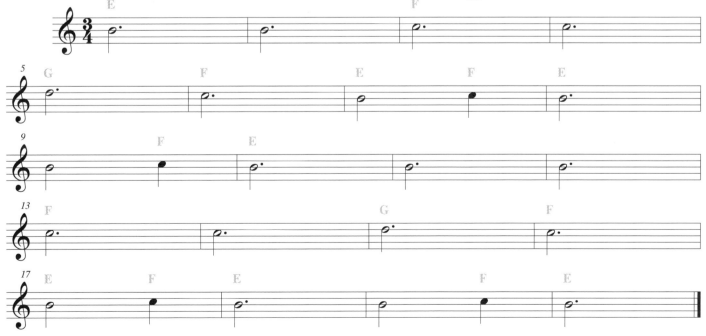

About Folk Music CD 1:26

Folk music is a broad term that applies to popular music that develops from a specific region or culture. Folk music is usually passed down from person to person—orally, from experienced musicians to novices—and aurally—by listening and imitating. Since folk music is passed down in this manner, it is constantly evolving and changing due to the creative impulses and new influences of each succeeding generation. The flamenco music discussed earlier is an example of Spanish folk music. In America, since the 1950s, folk music has been used to describe a style of guitar and vocal music based in the tradition of early American folk musicians such as Pete Seeger and Woody Guthrie. Often folk music in America is associated with protest music because many of the early folk songs protested harsh working conditions, war, and other social issues.

Some of the more popular musicians with strong folk music roots and influences are Bob Dylan, James Taylor, Arlo Guthrie (Woody's son), Joni Mitchell, Jewel, and the Dave Mathews band.

About Folk Guitars

Folk music can be played on any style guitar, but the instrument most closely associated with this style is the steel-string acoustic guitar. The steel strings give the guitar a bright, penetrating sound, very suitable for strumming. The guitars usually have mahogany or rosewood backs and sides and spruce tops. Steel-string guitars come in many shapes and sizes. The guitar shown here is a small-bodied instrument that tends to work nicely for intimate singer/songwriter, coffee house–style performances.

Following is a second guitar part for "Folk Song" (see page 17). Just like the "Flamenco Fantasy" duet part, this second guitar part is a **harmony** part that moves perfectly parallel to the original melody. This piece is written in the style of a simple folk song. Notice that it contains only C and G7 chords. In addition to learning the harmony part shown here, you should improvise a simple strummed accompaniment to the melody/harmony. Once you've learned this song, it should be played as a duet (melody and harmony) or even a trio (melody, harmony, and accompaniment chords).

Folk Song (Duet Part) CD 1:27

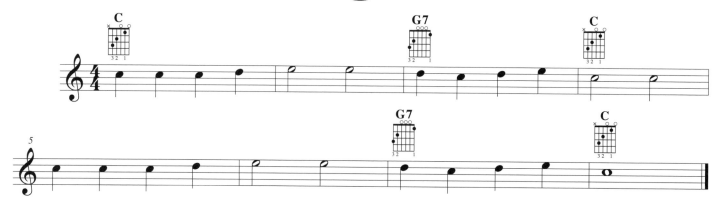

Harmony: Harmony is created when two or more notes are played at the same time. The example below shows the melody and the harmony line (the duet part) to "Folk Song" on one staff. Notice how the melody and the harmony move in perfect parallel motion. **This example is intended as an illustration only; you don't need to try to play it.**

Folk Song (Melody and Harmony Combined)

Jingle Bells CD 1:28

Brightly

J. PIERPONT

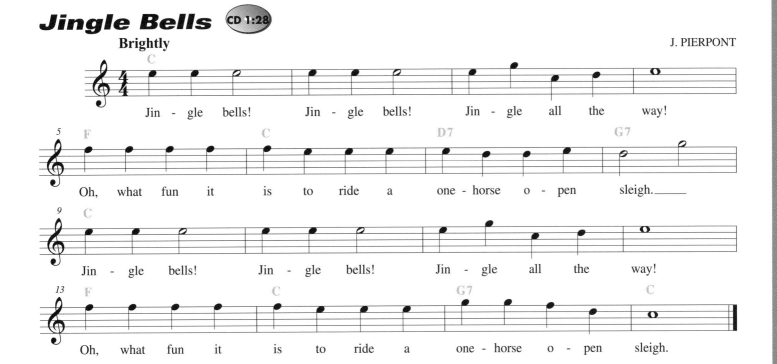

Jin - gle bells! Jin - gle bells! Jin - gle all the way!

Oh, what fun it is to ride a one - horse o - pen sleigh.____

Jin - gle bells! Jin - gle bells! Jin - gle all the way!

Oh, what fun it is to ride a one - horse o - pen sleigh.

tie:

A curved line connecting two notes of the same pitch is called a **tie.** Play the first note and hold it for the full value of both notes combined—do not pick the second note. "Saints" has tied notes in measures 2, 4, 8, 12, and 16.

quarter-note rest: 𝄽

This song introduces the quarter-note rest (𝄽). Make sure to count the rest (in this case it falls on beat 1 of the first measure), but don't play anything until the C on beat 2.

When the Saints Go Marching In CD 1:29

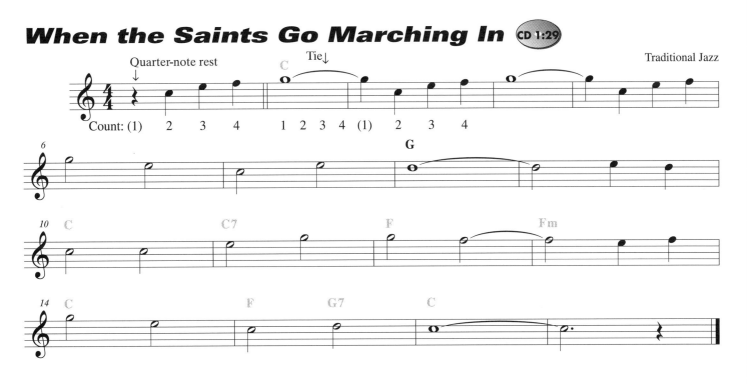

Traditional Jazz

Quarter-note rest   Tie↓

Count: (1) 2 3 4   1 2 3 4 (1) 2 3 4

New Rhythm

This is an eighth note: ♪ An eighth note receives one-half of a beat.

Two eighth notes equal one quarter note: ♫ = ♩

Single eighth notes are written like this: ♪

Groups of two or more eighth notes are beamed together: ♫♫

Counting Eighth Notes: In 4/4 time each measure is divided into four equal beats. Eighth notes divide each beat in half. A beat can be divided in half by saying "and" between each count.

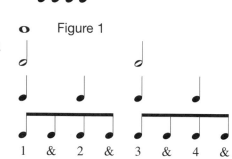

Figure 1

1 & 2 & 3 & 4 &

The Down-Up Stroke: The down-up stroke is one continuous movement—a note is played with a down-stroke, and then the next note is played with an up-stroke as the pick returns to playing position. The pick hand should swing freely from the wrist in a slight arc. Eighth notes are played with alternating down-up strokes—down on the counts (1 2 3 4) and up on "and." Tap your foot as you play—your foot taps on "1 2 3 4" and is up on the "and" of each beat.

Practice your down-up strokes with this next picking study. Hold your pick loosely; it should flow through the string easily. Count as you play.

Down-stroke: ⊓   Up-stroke: ⋁

Eighth-Note Picking Study

1 (&) 2 & 3 (&) 4 &   1 (&) 2 & 3 (&) 4 (&)   1 (&) 2 & 3 (&) 4 (&)   1 (&) 2 & 3 (&) 4 (&)

The Down-Up Strum

Strumming with a pick is perfect for creating strong rhythmic guitar accompaniments. Hold the pick **loosely** between your thumb and index finger when strumming. The pick should flow through the strings with very little resistance—if you hold the pick too tightly, it will strike the strings too hard and produce an ugly sound.

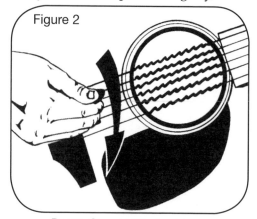

Down-Strum: All six strings

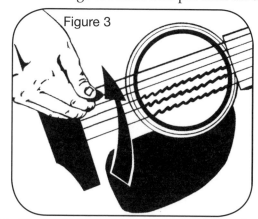

Up-Strum: Only the strings closest to the floor

To play a down-up strum: When strumming down and up, always swing your pick hand loosely, pivoting your forearm from the elbow. The pick should travel in a semi-circle, striking all the notes of the chord on the down-stroke but usually only the top strings (closest to the floor) on the up-stroke. Listen to the CD to hear how this strum should sound.

Practice "Strum Pattern 2" until you can play it smoothly, with a steady beat. When you are ready, play along with the CD.

Strum Pattern 2 CD 1:31

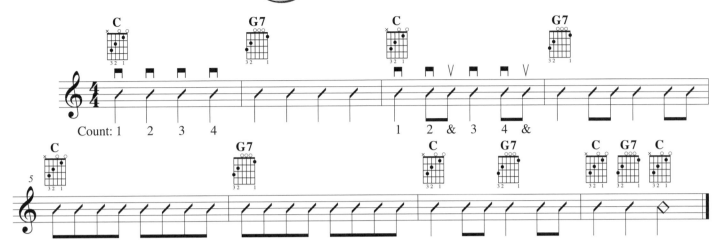

Now try playing the accompaniment/strumming part to "Folk Song." Here is "Folk Song" written out for guitar ensemble in three parts. Learn Guitar 3 (the strumming part) and then perform the song with friends and with the included recording.

Folk Song (Ensemble) CD 1:32

Strum Pattern 3: The Bass-Note Strum Pattern

This is a popular guitar strum pattern that applies to many styles of music. It is written in tab with rhythm notation included.

- Hold the full C chord. On beats 1 and 3, play just the bass note (5th string C) with the pick.

- On beats 2 and 4, strum the rest of the chord (strings 4–1).

- For the G7 chord, the pattern is the same: On beats 1 and 3, play the bass note (6th string G).

- On beats 2 and 4, strum the rest of the chord (strings 5–1).

- In bar 5 of the example, try using a down-up strum on beats 2 and 4. Remember, the up-strum should catch only the top strings.

- Listen to the CD to hear how this strum should sound, and then play along.

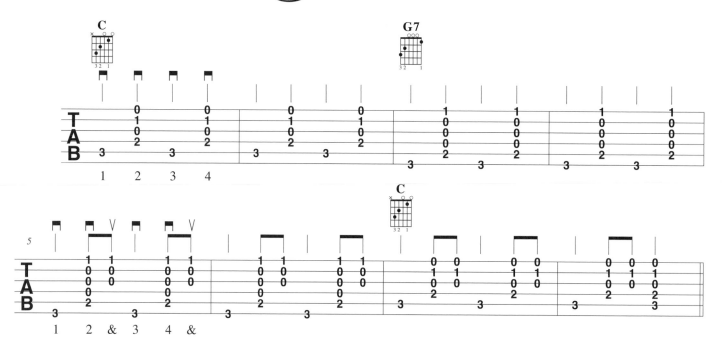

About "Jambalaya" and Cajun Music

"Jambalaya" is a classic song by country music legend Hank Williams. The song is written in the style of **Cajun music**—the folk music of French speaking residents of southern Louisiana (the New Orleans area, also known as Acadia). The French settled this area of Louisiana in the mid-1700s. The music of this region was originally French folk music, but as the French musicians mingled with the local musicians, the music evolved into what is now known as Cajun music. Cajun music is up-tempo dance music played to simple chord progressions. The bands often feature accordion and fiddle.

Listen to the recording to get a feel for the song. Improvise your own bass-note strum pattern as you play along with the CD. Then try to sing, or at least hum, the tune as you accompany yourself on the guitar. The chords are written above the lyrics. See the glossary on the next page for some of the Cajun words used in the lyrics. Verse 2 uses the same chords as the first verse. Use your ear to determine when to change chords in Verse 2.

Jambalaya CD 1:35

Words and Music by HANK WILLIAMS

Verse 1:

         C   G7
Goodbye Joe, me gotta go, me oh my oh.
                              C
Me gotta go pole the pirogue down the bayou.
                           G7
My Yvonne, the sweetest one, me oh my oh.
                           C
Son of a gun we'll have big fun on the bayou.

Chorus:

                           G7
Jambalaya and a crawfish pie and file gumbo.
                         C
'Cause tonight I'm gonna see my ma cher amio.
                G7
Pick guitar, fill fruit jar and be gay-o.
                      C
Son of a gun we'll have big fun on the bayou.

Verse 2:

Thibodaux, Fontaineaux, the place is buzzin'.

Kin folk come to see Yvonne by the dozen.

Dress in style, go hog wild, me oh my oh.

Son of a gun we'll have big fun on the bayou.

(To Chorus:)

GLOSSARY

pirogue (PEE-rohg)   A type of canoe that is propelled through shallow waterways with a long pole.

bayou (BI-yoo)   The shallow marshes and bodies of water weaving throughout the Acadia region.

jambalaya (juhm-buh-LI-uh)   A popular spicy Cajun stew. The ingredients change depending on what is available.

file gumbo (fill-A GUM-boh)   A traditional spicy Acadian stew.

Artist Portrait: Hank Williams

Born in Alabama September 17, 1923, Hiram (Hank) Williams was small and fragile and may have gravitated toward music as an alternative to sports. In 1949 he made his national debut on the stage of the Grand Ole Opry in Nashville, Tennessee. He passed away a brief five years later, in 1953, but the legacy of those five short years has influenced every succeeding generation of musicians. Although he is widely considered one of the founders of modern country music, his influence on rock-and-roll and other music styles is very strong. Artists outside the country music genre who have covered his songs include George Thorogood (blues), Norah Jones (jazz), and Elvis Presley. Hank Williams' songs are the backbone of the standard country music repertoire, and his personality and stage presence helped define the modern image of a music superstar.

© Underwood & Underwood / CORBIS

Traditional Jazz

Jazz evolved in New Orleans in the early 1900s. The music is upbeat and lively, and features a group-style improvisation in which several members of the band simultaneously create new melodies and countermelodies weaving in and around the original melody. Traditional jazz groups usually featured a banjo instead of a guitar because the banjo's loud, bright sound could be heard above the horn players.

NEW CONTENT

Melodic
New Notes on the 3rd String: G and A
Ear Training
Songs:
 "Plaisir d'Amour"
 "Ode to Joy"
 "Singing Strings"
 "Danny Boy"

Chordal
Key of G/**I, IV,** and **V7** Chords
G, D, and D7 Chords
Three-Chord Rock-and-Roll:
 The "Wild Thing" Pattern
 The "Sloopy" Pattern
Introducing Fingerpicking/
 Fingerpicking Pattern 1
Song: "Silent Night"
Improvising and Ear Training:
 "The Sloop John B."
Three-Chord Song List

Theory
Chord Tones
Stylistic
About Traditional Jazz
Swing Feel
Blue Notes
Song:
 "When the Saints Go Marching In" (Duet)

NEW VOCABULARY

blue notes: Dissonant notes that the early blues singers would use to bring a gritty feel to the music

swing feel: The way jazz musicians interpret eighth notes in an uneven galloping rhythm

traditional jazz: An early style of jazz that evolved in New Orleans in the early 1900s

The Notes on the 3rd String CD 1:36

New Notes: G and A

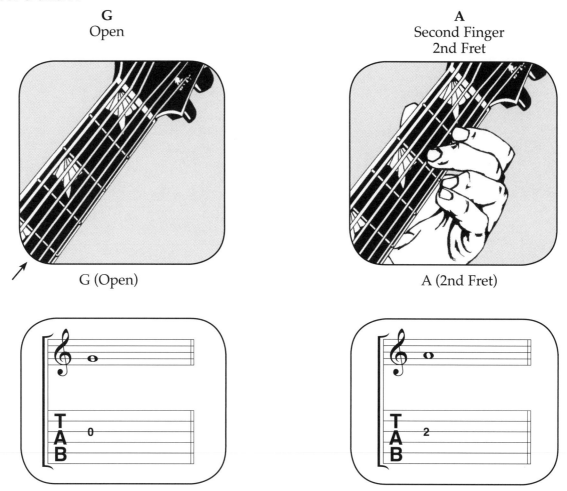

Example 1: This example uses eighth notes (review page 30). Use up-strokes and down-strokes as indicated above the music.

Example 2

Ear Training   CD 1:37

Example 1: Sing and then play: Do, Ti, La, Sol (C, B, A, G)

Example 2: Sing and then play: from Sol to Sol (G, A, B, C, D, E, F, G)

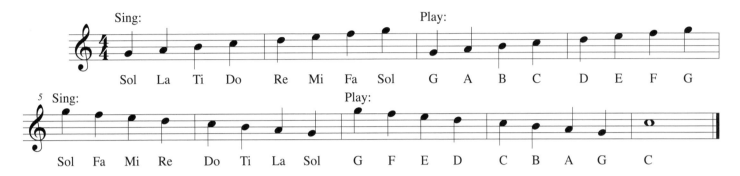

Originally a French operatic song, "Plaisir d'Amour" is so popular that it has been passed on into the folk and popular music genres. The song was set to new lyrics and recorded by Elvis Presley as "Can't Help Falling in Love." It became his forty-sixth top-40 hit.

Plaisir d'Amour   CD 1:38

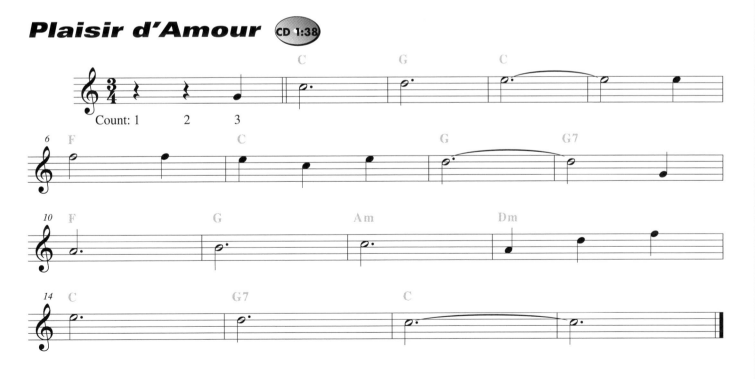

On page 22 you learned that C and G7 are the **I** and the **V7** chords in the key of C. Following is a G major scale. As you can see, in the key of G, G is the **I** chord, C is the **IV** chord, and D is the **V** chord. Notice that the scale is numbered with Roman numerals.

G	A	B	C	D	E	F♯	G
I	II	III	IV	V	VI	VII	VIII

The three most important chords in any key are always the **I, IV,** and **V** chords of that key. In the previous section you learned the C chord. Here are the G **(I)**, D **(V)**, and D7 **(V7)** chords. (Sometimes the **V** chord [D] is used, and sometimes the **V7** [D7] is used.)

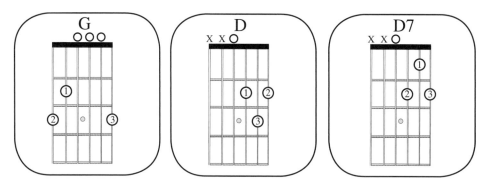

To play the G chord:

- Place your second finger on the 6th string, just behind the 3rd fret.
- Place your first finger on the 5th string, just behind the 2nd fret.
- Place your third finger on the 1st string, just behind the 3rd fret.
- The 4th, 3rd, and 2nd strings are played open.

To play the D chord:

- Place your first finger on the 3rd string, just behind the 2nd fret.
- Place your second finger on the 1st string, just behind the 2nd fret.
- Place your third finger on the 2nd string, just behind the 3rd fret.
- The 4th string is played open.

To play the D7 chord:

- Place your second finger on the 3rd string, just behind the 2nd fret.
- Place your first finger on the 2nd string, just behind the 1st fret.
- Place your third finger on the 1st string, just behind the 2nd fret.
- The 4th string is played open.

Practice each chord. Strum through the chord and try to get a clear sound with all the notes ringing.

Key Signature: The F♯ indicated at the beginning of this song tells you that you are in the key of G and that all F notes are sharp. You'll learn more about keys and key signatures later.

Example 1: Combining the Chords CD 1:40

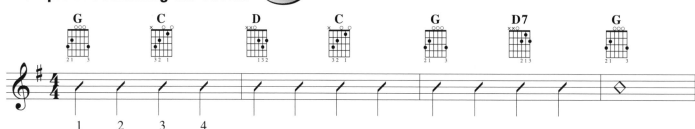

Three-Chord Rock-and-Roll

You will hear the expression "three-chord rock-and-roll" often. It refers to songs based entirely on the **I**, **IV**, and **V** chords—and there are hundreds of them. Following are some examples of rock-and-roll classics based on the **I**, **IV**, and **V** chords. The main difference between the guitar parts for these songs is the strumming rhythm.

The following examples may seem challenging at first. You won't learn to play them smoothly at tempo in just a few hours. But stick with it—in a few weeks you can master these patterns and you'll be well on your way to playing some great songs.

The following example uses the rhythm from the Troggs song "Wild Thing." Use all down-strokes for the strum (it is common for rock guitarists to use all down-strokes for rhythms like this). Listen to the recording and play along. The counting is shown below. Notice the **eighth-note rest** on beat 3 and the **repeat sign** at the end.

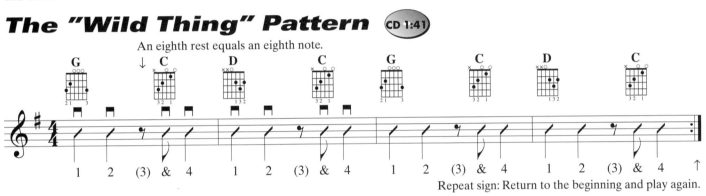

The next example uses the rhythm from "Hang On Sloopy." You can see how similar this one is to "Wild Thing." This one is played at a medium tempo. All down-strokes are suggested for a good solid feel; as an option, try alternate strumming as well.

The prelude to "Ode to Joy," the fourth movement of Ludwig van Beethoven's Ninth Symphony, was inspired by Friedrich von Schiller's poem "An die Freude," known in English as "Ode to Joy," and written in 1785. The Ninth Symphony was first performed May 7, 1824, in Vienna. By that time Beethoven was totally deaf. He was able to write the music that he heard in his head even though he could not hear it with his ears. In 1972 this beautiful melody was adopted by the European Union as its official anthem.

Here is the first verse of this melody. The melody is played on the 2nd and 3rd strings. An English translation of the original poem has been included.

Ode to Joy CD 1:43

Text by FRIEDRICH VON SCHILLER
Music by LUDWIG VAN BEETHOVEN

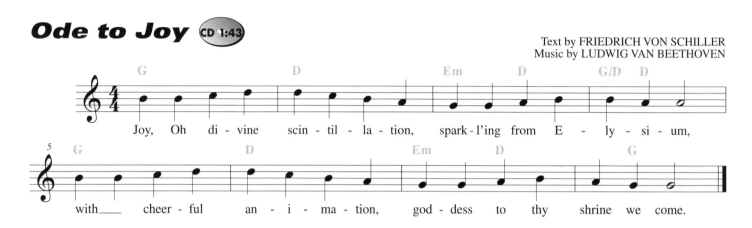

In the next song, allow each note to continue to ring for the entire measure. Keep your fingers curved while playing the fretted notes so that they do not stop the other strings from ringing. Do not lift your fingers from the notes until absolutely necessary.

Singing Strings CD 1:44

New Note: High A CD 1:45

A
Fourth Finger
5th Fret

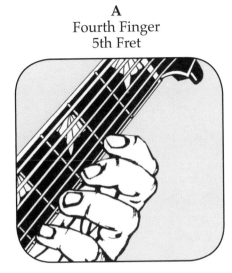

The high A is played on the 1st string, at the 5th fret, with the fourth finger.

Ledger lines are used for notes that lie above or below the staff. The high A is placed on the first ledger line above the staff.

A (5th Fret)

"Danny Boy" is a popular Irish folk song with a beautiful and melancholy melody. Notice the high A note played in measures 3, 6, and 11.

Danny Boy CD 1:46

Irish Folk Song

Slowly, with feeling

Oh, Dan - ny Boy, the pipes, the pipes are call - ing..._____ From glen to glen, and down the moun - tain side._____ The sum - mer's gone, and all the ros - es fall - ing..._____ it's you, it's you must go and I must bide.

Strumming with a pick is perfect for creating strong, rhythmic guitar accompaniments. In contrast, you can also create beautiful, lush-sounding accompaniments by using your right-hand fingers to pluck the notes of a chord individually.

Right-hand fingering indications: thumb = p; index finger = i; middle finger = m; ring finger = a

Fingerpicking Pattern 1

- This pattern is written in tab only since you haven't learned to read all the notes in these chords yet. It is common to find guitar music written in tab only.

- Hold the indicated chord and place your index, middle and ring fingers on the top three strings (the three closest to the floor). Place your thumb on the bass note (6th string for the G chord, 5th string for the C chord, and 4th string for the D7).

- The pattern is *p i m a m i* and is counted *1 and 2 and 3 and*.

- Play the last chord by brushing your thumb through the top four strings.

- Listen to the CD. Try to play along with it.

Fingerpicking Pattern 1

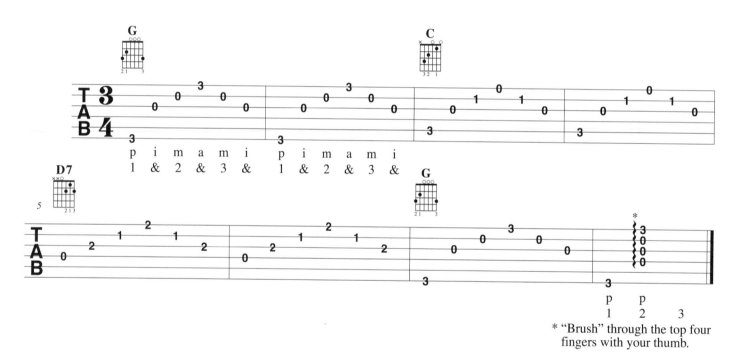

* "Brush" through the top four fingers with your thumb.

Finer Points of Technique

- Position your right hand by resting your right elbow on top of the guitar. Relax and dangle your right hand in front of the sound hole (or pickups on an electric guitar). Now pivot your whole forearm so that the palm of your hand faces the strings. Keep your wrist arched, not flattened.

- All right-hand finger motion is from the knuckle at your palm, not the upper finger joints. Push your finger through the string and straight toward the palm of your hand.

- When plucking with the "a" finger, your little finger also moves—as if they were taped together.

- Your thumb should remain straight and should move from its base.

†CD Track 48 contains samples of a variety of fingerpicking guitarists.

Now apply the previous fingerpicking pattern to each of the chords in "Silent Night." Try to sing the song and accompany yourself, and definitely play along with the included recording. Also, notice that tablature is not included; simply apply the previous pattern to each of the chords shown throughout the music.

Note The melody is included for reference only (which is why the notes are gray, not black). It contains notes and rhythms you have not learned yet, so simply play the chords and sing or hum the melody.

Silent Night CD 1:50

Traditional

Si - lent night, ho - ly night,

all is calm, all is bright.

'Round yon Vir - gin Moth - er and Child,

Ho - ly In - fant so ten - der and mild,

sleep in heav - en - ly peace,_____

sleep_____ in heav - en - ly peace._____

"The Sloop John B." uses only three chords: **I, IV,** and **V7** (G, C, and D7). The chords have not been indicated, only the lyrics. (The first chord, G, is indicated for you.) You will try to figure out when to change chords for yourself. Try one of the following:

- Sing the song to yourself, begin on the G chord, strum along, and try to figure out when to change from the G to the next chord.

- Have a friend or teacher strum and sing the song. Listen and raise your hand when you think the chord should change.

- The song is sung on the CD, strum along. Let your ear guide you to change chords.

- Once you are confidant that you know when a chord change occurs, write the chord above the lyric on which the change happens.

The Sloop John B.

Traditional

Verse 1:

     G

We come on the sloop *John B.*,

My grandfather and me.

'Round Nassau town we did roam.

Drinking all night,

We got into a fight;

I feel so broke up,

I wanna go home.

Chorus:

So, hoist up the *John B.*'s sails.

See how the mainsail sets.

Send for the captain ashore, let me go home.

Let me go home, please let me go home.

I feel so broke up, I wanna go home.

Verse 2:

The poor cook he got the fits,

Ate up all of the grits.

Then he took and threw away all of the corn.

Sheriff John Stone,

Please leave me alone,

I feel so broke up,

I wanna go home.

(To Chorus:)

Verse 3:

The first mate, he got drunk.

Broke up the people's trunk.

Constable had to come and take him away.

Sheriff John Stone,

Please leave me alone,

This is the worst trip

I ever been on.

(To Chorus:)

Following is a list of songs that use only the **I, IV,** and **V7** chords. Pick a song you know and try to sing the melody while accompanying yourself on the guitar. Make up your own strum pattern and use your ear to figure out when to change chords.

Three-Chord Songs

"Amazing Grace"

"Danny Boy"

"Deck the Halls"

"Jingle Bells"

"Silent Night"

"Home on the Range"

"Red River Valley"

"Oh, Susanna"

"Molly Malone"

"On Top of Old Smoky"

"Margaritaville"

"This Train"

Chord Tones: You can always figure out the notes in the **I, IV,** and **V** chords by writing out the notes in the related major scale; then, starting on the root of each chord, count up to the 3rd and 5th notes from the root (every other note). Make sure to count the root as "1."

For example: A "G" chord would be G–B–D:

1	2	**3**	4	**5**			
G	A	**B**	C	**D**	E	F♯	G

A "C" chord would be C–E–G:

			1	2	**3**	4	**5**
G	A	B	**C**	D	**E**	F♯	**G**

A "D" chord would be D–F♯–A (notice that the scale has been extended):

				1	2	**3**	4	**5**
G	A	B	C	**D**	E	**F♯**	G	**A**

D7 would add the next chord tone above the 5th:

	1	2	**3**	4	**5**	6	**7**
G	A	B	C	**D**	E	**F♯**	G	**A**	B	**C**

Following is the C major scale. Use this scale to fill in the blanks below.

C major:

C	D	E	F	G	A	B	C
I	II	III	IV	V	VI	VII	VIII

In the key of C, what are the **I, IV,** and **V** chords? _____ _____ _____

What are the notes in the **I** chord? _____

What are the notes in the **IV** chord? _____

What are the notes in the **V** and **V7** chords? _____ _____

Using the following four chord diagrams for reference, fill in the blank tab. The first one is done for you.

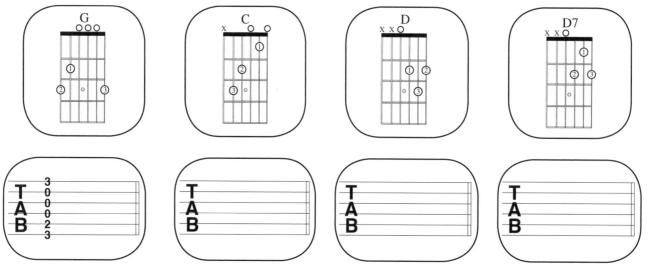

SECTION 4 • Chord Tones

About Traditional Jazz

Traditional jazz evolved in New Orleans in the early 1900s. The music is up-beat and lively and features a group style of improvisation in which several members of the band simultaneously improvise new melodies and countermelodies weaving in and around the original melody. Early jazz groups usually featured a banjo instead of a guitar because the banjo's loud, bright sound could be heard above the horn players. Listen to the CD to hear an example of early jazz.

Swing Feel

It is often said that jazz music swings. Swing is a musical feel that is lively and rhythmic. It also changes the way eighth notes are interpreted. The basic or most common rhythm in jazz melodies is the eighth note. Early jazz set it self apart from folk and classical music by interpreting the eighth-note melodies unevenly, or long-short. Listen to CD Track 53 to hear the following examples of even eighth notes (also called straight eighth notes) and uneven eighth notes (also called swing eighth notes).

Straight eighth notes are played evenly: Swing eighth notes are played long-short (gallop):

Swing Example 1

Swing eighth notes are written exactly like straight eighth notes (evenly). A swing indication is usually placed at the beginning of the song to show that the eighth notes are to be played swing style. Listen to CD Track 53 to hear this example played straight and then with a swing feel.

Play with a straight eighth-note feel:

Swing Example 2

Here is the opening phrase of "When the Saints Go Marchin' In" interpreted as a jazz musicain might, with a swinging eighth-note melody.

Play with a swing eighth-note feel:

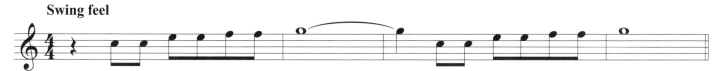

Blue Notes CD 1:54

Another thing that sets jazz apart from folk and classical music is the use of **blue notes**. Blue notes come from blues music. They are dissonant notes that early blues singers used to bring a grittier feel to the music.

"When the Saints Go Marchin' In" uses several blue notes: G-sharp (G♯), A-sharp (A♯), and D-sharp (D♯).

A sharp sign (♯) raises a note one half step—the distance from one fret to the next:

"When the Saints Go Marchin' In" is one of the more popular examples of traditional jazz.

- In this duet arrangement, Guitar 1 plays a jazz-style version of the melody. You already played the basic melody on page 29.

- Guitar 2 is the harmony part. In this case, some of Guitar 2 is traditional parallel harmony (see measures 6–7 and 11–13) and some of it is **countermelody**—a part that fills the spaces between the melody phrases (measures 2–5 and 8–9).

- Look for the blue notes in the countermelody. Remember to play this piece with a swing feel.

- Learn both parts. Play the song with a friend and with the included recording.

When the Saints Go Marchin' In (Duet) CD 1:55

Traditional Jazz

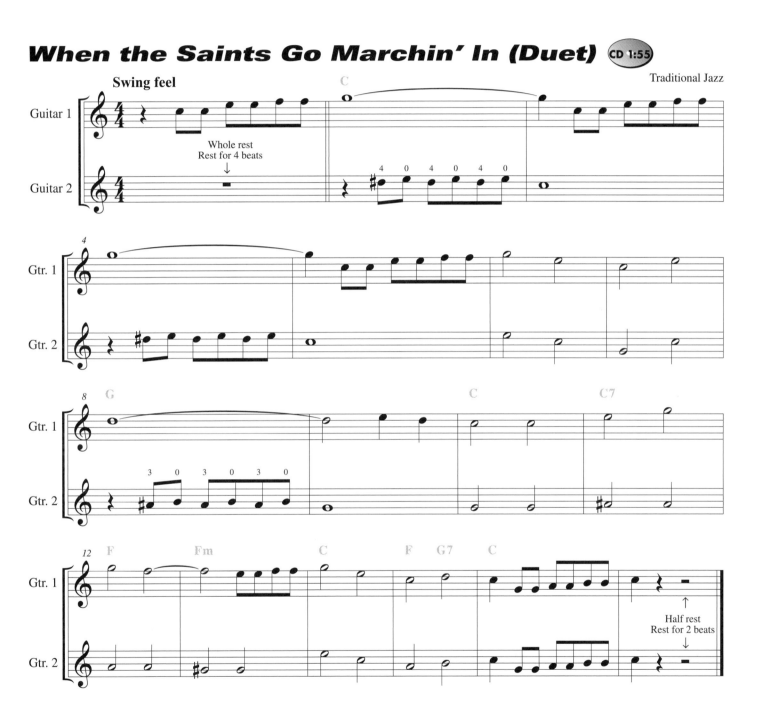

Rock and Roll
In the early 1950s, young musicians began mixing elements of country music with rhythm and blues.
The result is rock and roll.

NEW CONTENT

Melodic
New Notes on the 4th String: E, F, and G
Songs:
"Spy to Spy"
"Amazing Grace" (Duet)
Form Indications: Repeat Signs,
1st and 2nd Endings

Theory
Scale Construction
Theory Review Worksheet
Major Scale Construction Worksheet
Ear Training
Fingerboard Diagram Worksheet
Songs:
"Plaisir d'Amour" (Duet)
"Menuet in G" (Ensemble)

Chordal
Key of D: **I, IV** and **V7** Chords
D, G, A, and A7 Chords
Fingerpicking Patterns 2 and 3
Three-Chord Rock-and-Roll:
"Wild Thing" Pattern
"Twist and Shout" Pattern

Stylistic
About Rock-and-Roll
Artist Profile: Les Paul
Classic Rock Riffs in D

NEW VOCABULARY

repeat sign ( ):   Indicates to go back and play the music again

section repeat: ( ):   When a section of music falls between two facing repeat signs, repeat
                               that section once

1st and 2nd endings: Play the 1st ending, repeat the section, and play only the 2nd
                               ending the second time

riff: A short, catchy, repetitive figure that often forms the basis for a song or
                               for a guitar part

half step: The distance from a note to the next closest note (C to C♯, C♯ to D, D to
                               D♯, etc.). This is the same as the distance from one fret to the next

whole step: Equal to two half steps. This is the same as a two-fret distance.

key signature: Sharps or flats immediately following the clef that are used to indicate
                               which notes are altered throughout the piece

shuffle: Uneven eighth-note feel; similar to swing feel

The Notes on the 4th String

New Notes: D, E, and F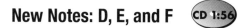

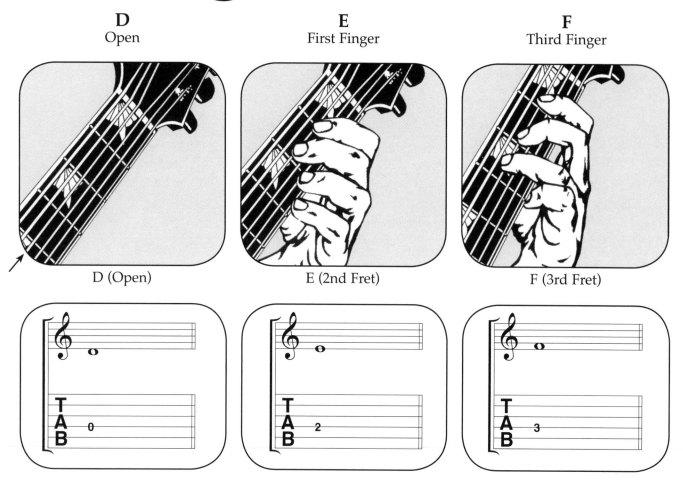

D — Open — D (Open)

E — First Finger — E (2nd Fret)

F — Third Finger — F (3rd Fret)

Example 1

Example 2: This example reviews all of the notes on the first four strings. Use strict alternate picking.

Example 3

"Spy to Spy" is a good opportunity to practice your 4th-string notes. Practice the song with both strict alternate picking and all down-strokes. The alternate picking is critical for developing speed, but the down-strokes can provide a nice driving rhythmic feel for medium tempos.

Spy to Spy CD 1:57

"Amazing Grace" uses the notes on the first four strings and the G, C, and D chords. Use Fingerpicking Pattern 1 (from page 42) to play the accompaniment part to this song. Play this as a duet. Learn both the melody and the accompaniment and play each with a friend or the included recording.

Form Indications

repeat sign (:‖):	Indicates to go back and play the music again
repeat of a section (‖: :‖):	When a section of music falls between two facing repeat signs, repeat that section once.
1st and 2nd endings:	Play the 1st ending, repeat the section, and play only the 2nd ending the second time. See the end of "Amazing Grace."

Amazing Grace (Duet) CD 1:58

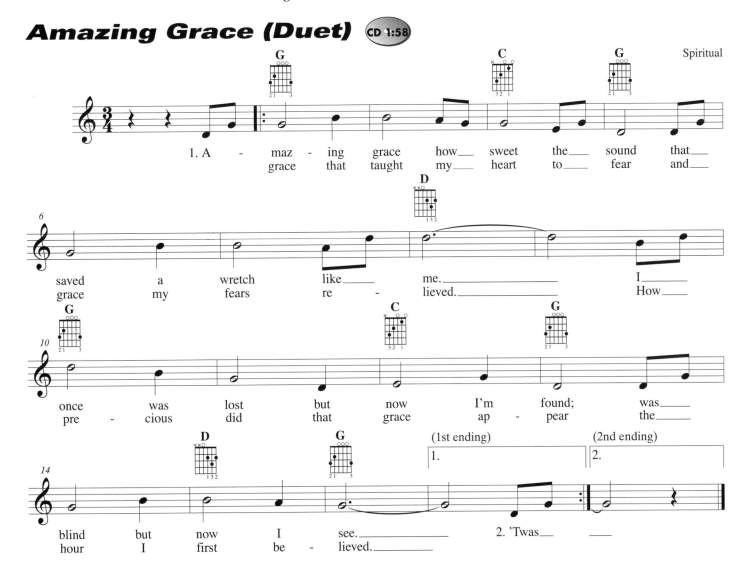

Part 1: Review

You can figure out the notes in the **I, IV,** and **V** chords by writing out the notes in the related major scale; then, starting on the root of each chord, count up to the 3rd and 5th notes from the root (every other note). Make sure to count the root as "1." (Review page 46 if necessary.)

Following is the D major scale. Use the notes of this scale to fill in the blanks.

D major scale:

D   E   F♯   G   A   B   C♯   D

In the key of D what are the **I, IV,** and **V** chords? _____   _____   _____

What are the notes in the **I** chord? _____

What are the notes in the **IV** chord? _____

What are the notes in the **V** and **V7** chords? _____   _____

Part 2: Major Scale Construction Worksheet

half step: The distance from a note to the next closest note (C to C♯, C♯ to D, D to D♯, etc.). This is the same as the distance from one fret to the next.

whole step: Equal to two half steps. This is the same as a two-fret distance.

C major scale:

	C♯/D♭		D♯/E♭			F♯/G♭		G♯/A♭		A♯/B♭		
C		D		E	F		G		A		B	C
	1		1	1/2	1		1		1		1/2	

Notice in the C major scale above that all adjacent natural (not sharp or flat) notes are a whole step apart (1), except E–F and B–C, which are both natural half steps (1/2).

Using that information, fill in the whole steps and half steps for the following G and D major scales by writing "1" or "1/2" in the following blanks:

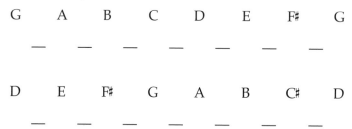

G   A   B   C   D   E   F♯   G

—   —   —   —   —   —   —

D   E   F♯   G   A   B   C♯   D

—   —   —   —   —   —   —

Below are the notes from A to A. Write the appropriate sharp signs to make the notes match the pattern of whole steps and half steps. When filled in correctly, this is an A major scale:

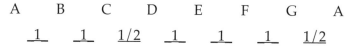

A   B   C   D   E   F   G   A
_1_ _1_ _1/2_ _1_ _1_ _1_ _1/2_

Just as a sharp sign raises a note by one half step, a flat sign (♭) lowers a note by one half step. Below are the notes from F to F. The F major scale contains one flat (♭). Using the indicated pattern of whole steps and half steps, indicate which note is flat:

F   G   A   B   C   D   E   F
_1_ _1_ _1/2_ _1_ _1_ _1_ _1/2_

Ear Training CD 1:59

As you have already seen, the G scale contains an F#. Sing and then play the G major scale. (Remember: A sharp sign raises a note one half step, so F# is one fret higher than F: 1st string/2nd fret.)

Example 1

Sing: / Play:

Do Re Mi Fa Sol La Ti Do

Sing: / Play:

Do Ti La Sol Fa Mi Re Do

Part 3: Fingerboard Diagrams Worksheet

As discussed, major scales follow this pattern of whole (1) and half (1/2) steps: 1, 1, 1/2, 1, 1, 1, 1/2. Shown below is a neck diagram of a C major scale played on one string. Notice the pattern of whole steps (two frets) and half steps (one fret):

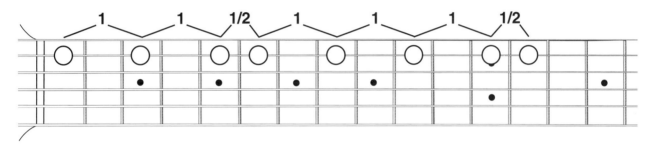

On the diagram below, draw a G major scale on the 3rd string starting on the open G note. After you draw the scale, play it using one finger. If you have done it correctly, it will sound like Do, Re, Mi, Fa, Sol, La, Ti, Do.

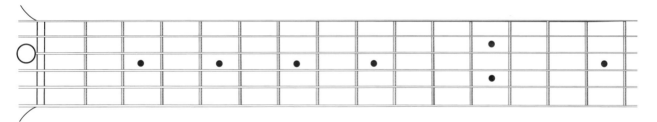

On the diagram below, draw a D major scale on the 4th string starting on the open D note. After you draw the scale, play it using one finger.

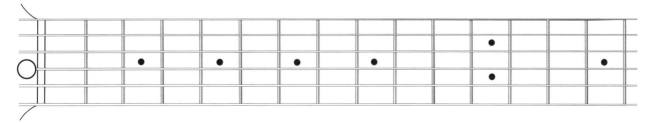

Now pick any note on any string and play a major scale on only that string with the selected note as the root.

Key Signature: A **key signature** is indicated by the sharps or flats placed immediately following the clef used to indicate which notes are altered throughout the piece.

Key of G: In the key of G, all F notes are sharp (just like in the G major scale). Rather than placing a sharp sign before every F, the F# is indicated in the key signature at the beginning of the staff. So, a sharp sign on the top line of the staff (where F is written) indicates that all Fs are sharp and that the song is in the key of G.

On page 37 you learned "Plaisir d'Amour" in the key of C. Here it is in the key of G. This is a good example of how you can play the same song in different keys. Learn the melody (notice the F# in the key signature) and the chord accompaniment. Following are three possible ways to play the accompaniment. Learn each. Also try to improvise your own variations on these patterns.

Example 1:
Fingerpicking Pattern 1

Example 2:
Quarter-Note Strum Pattern

Example 3:
Bass Note/Strum Pattern

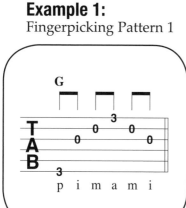

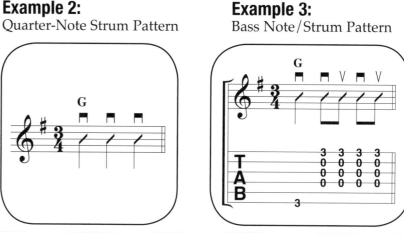

Plaisir d'Amour (Duet) CD 1:61

French Folk Song

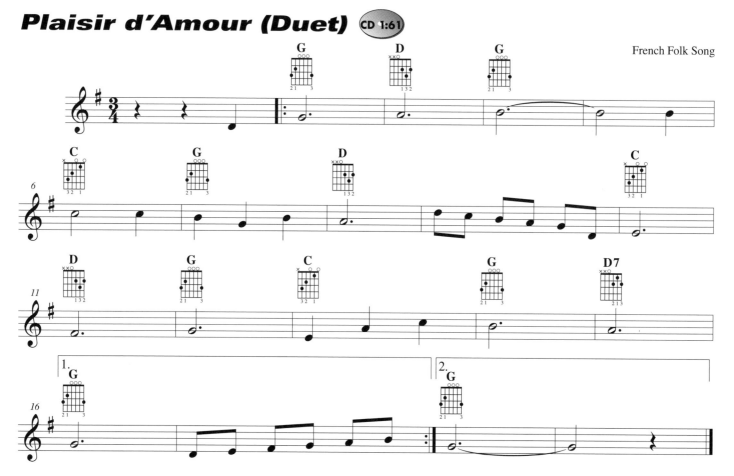

SECTION 5 • "Plaisir d'Amour"

Following is a D major scale. As you can see, in the key of D, D is the **I** chord, G is the **IV** chord, A is the **V** chord, and A7 is the **V7** chord.

D	E	F♯	*G*	*A*	B	C♯	D
I	**II**	**III**	**IV**	**V**	**VI**	**VII**	**VIII**

As you have already learned, the three most important chords in any key are always the **I**, **IV**, and **V** chords of that key. In previous sections you learned the D and G chords. Below are the A (**V**) and A7 (**V7**) chords. Again, sometimes the **V** chord (A) is used, and sometimes the **V7** chord (A7) is used. You can always experiment to see which sounds better to you for the song you are playing.

Strum through each chord and try to get a clear sound with all the notes ringing. On the A7 chord make sure that the open 3rd string G is loud and clear, not accidentally muted by your second finger.

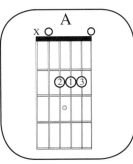

To play the A chord:
- Place your second finger on the 4th string, just behind the 2nd fret.
- Place your first finger on the 3rd string, just behind the 2nd fret.
- Place your third finger on the 2nd string, just behind the 2nd fret.
- The 5th and 1st strings are played open.

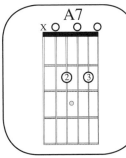

To play the A7 chord:
- Place your second finger on the 4th string, just behind the 2nd fret.
- Place your third finger on the 2nd string, just behind the 2nd fret.
- The 5th, 3rd, and 1st strings are played open.

The next example introduces two new fingerpicking patterns you can use to practice these chords. Notice the key signature: F♯ and C♯ indicate the key of D (same as the D major scale).

Fingerpicking Pattern 2: p i m i p i m i—Your thumb (p) always plucks the bottom note of the chord, your index finger (i) always plucks the 3rd string, and your middle finger (m) always plucks the 2nd string.

Fingerpicking Pattern 3: p i a i p i a i—This pattern is a variation of Fingerpicking Pattern 2. Use your ring finger (a) to pluck the 1st string instead of your middle finger to pluck the 2nd string.

Example 1: Fingerpicking Pattern 2 CD 1:63

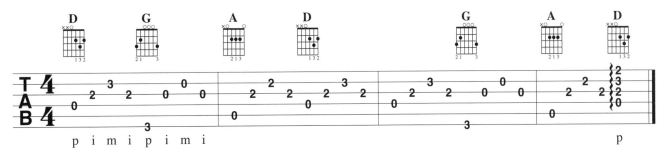

Example 2: Fingerpicking Pattern 3 CD 1:64

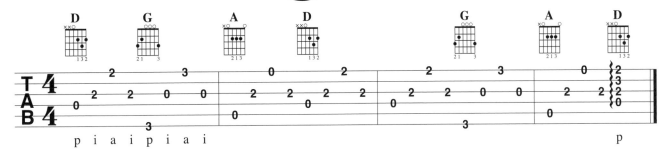

On page 39 you learned several three-chord rock and roll guitar parts in G. Many rock-and-roll songs are based on just the **I**, **IV**, and **V** chords. Now try a few in the key of D. These may seem hard at first, but stick with it.

Here is the "Wild Thing" rhythm pattern in the key of D. Use all down-strokes for the strum.

The "Wild Thing" Pattern   CD 1:65

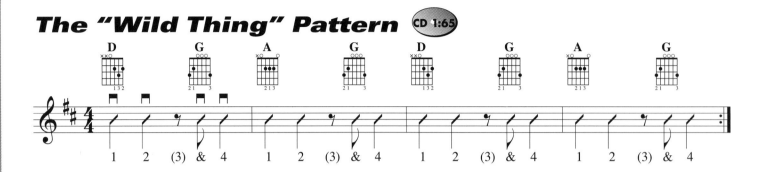

This next example uses the rhythm from the Beatles' version of "Twist and Shout." This one is usually played faster than the previous example. Use down- and up-strokes as indicated. Notice the rest on beat 4. Keep a constant down-up strumming motion and "miss" the strings (a down-stroke) on beat 4, which puts you in position to play the A chord with an up-stroke on the "and" of 4.

The "Twist and Shout" Pattern   CD 1:66

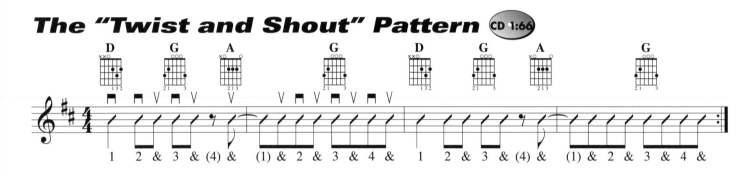

Important: Now apply the "Sloopy" pattern to the key of D (review page 39). Next, apply the "Twist and Shout" rhythm pattern to the **I**, **IV**, and **V** chords in the key of G. The more you practice strumming, the easier it gets.

Johann Sebastian Bach

As discussed, the **I, IV,** and **V** chords are the most important chords in any key and many songs are based only those three chords. Below is a guitar ensemble arrangement of "Menuet in G" from Johann Sebastian Bach's *Notebook for Anna Magdalena Bach.* You can see that even Bach based some of his songs on only three chords. Learn all three of the guitar parts and play along with the recording. Also get some friends together and play it as a trio.

Menuet in G (Ensemble) CD 1:67

J. S. BACH

About Rock-and-Roll

Until the early 1950s, the music industry was segregated, with black music and white music played on different radio stations and recorded on different record labels. But the airwaves couldn't be segregated, so young white and black musicians began to be influenced by what they heard on the various radio stations. These young musicians started experimenting with songs that combined black R&B and white country music. Meanwhile, Sam Philips, a young record producer and the owner of Sun Records, a label devoted to promoting rural southern musicians, began searching for artists who could help him make black R&B popular with white audiences. Sam Philips had good taste, or phenomenal luck, and within a few years he discovered Carl Perkins, Jerry Lee Lewis, Elvis Presley, and Johnny Cash.

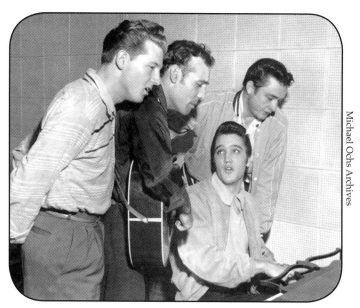

The "Million Dollar Quartet," from left to right: Jerry Lee Lewis, Carl Perkins, Elvis Presley, and Johnny Cash.

"Classic Rock Riffs in D" includes four variations on an extremely popular guitar bass-line riff (a riff is a repeated instrumental part). This example will give you lots of practice using F♯. Use strict alternating down-up strokes. Notice that even though these riffs are in the key of D (see the key signature), they each use the F-natural note (review "Blue Notes" on page 48).

These riffs can be played with straight eighth notes or with swing eighths (review page 47). In rock and blues, swing feel is called **shuffle.** Usually rock-and-roll songs with a straight-eighth feel are played pretty fast; shuffle grooves are usually at slower tempos. Both are demonstrated on the CD. Use the indicated left-hand fingerings. These fingerings place you in the 2nd position: the first finger is at the 2nd fret, the second finger is at the 3rd fret, and so on.

Classic Rock Riffs in D

Straight-Eighth Feel: CD 1:69   Shuffle Feel: CD 1:70

SECTION 5 • Rock-and-Roll

60

Artist Portrait: Les Paul

Les Paul was born in 1915 and went on to become one of the most popular guitarists of the 1940s and 1950s. Although Les Paul's guitar playing is stunningly brilliant and has influenced guitarists the world over, he is not a rock guitarist. So why has he been honored by every major rock organization, including induction into the Rock and Roll Hall of Fame in 2003? Because not one, but two of his inventions changed the sound of popular music forever. In 1941 Les patented the first solid-body electric guitar, called "The Log." The Log (shown at right, inset) consisted of one solid piece of wood forming the neck and the main body with two pickups mounted on top. Les then sawed the "wings" off of a hollow-body guitar and attached them to make the instrument look more like a regular guitar. In 1952 Gibson Musical Instruments launched the ultimate refinement of Les's design: the Les Paul guitar. This new instrument changed the way guitarists functioned within a band and ultimately changed the sound of popular music. Les's other invention, though less well known, equally affected the music industry. Funded by the era's greatest crooner and movie star, Bing Crosby, Les invented the first multi-track recording machine, which paved the way for the entire modern recording industry.

© William Coupon/CORBIS

About Rock-and-Roll Guitars

Although many rock-and-roll singers would accompany themselves with an acoustic steel-string guitar, the electric guitar came to define the sound of rock-and-roll and all rock music since. The first electric guitars started to become popular with jazz and blues guitarists in the 1940s, but the advent of loud rock-and-roll gave the solid-body electric guitar a life of its own. Because of the loud volume of rock-and-roll music, the solid-body electric guitar became a necessity—you couldn't hear an acoustic guitar over the band, and both hollow-body electrics and acoustic guitars with pick-ups (the electronics used to amplify the guitar, similar to a microphone) tended to produce feedback—a loud shrieking sound that occurs when an acoustic guitar is amplified too loudly. The first, and still the most, popular electric guitars were the Fender Stratocaster™, the Fender Telecaster™, the Gibson Les Paul™, and the Gibson 335™. (Although the Gibson 335 looks like a hollow-body guitar, it has a solid block of wood down the center of the body to prevent feedback.)

Gibson Les Paul™   Gibson 335™   Fender Stratocaster™   Fender Telecaster™

Classical Guitar
Very few of the early classical performers and composers considered the guitar a "serious" instrument. It was not until Andrés Segovia established the classical guitar as an instrument capable of communicating the subtleties and complexities of the classical repertoire that the guitar began to be taken seriously as a concert instrument.

NEW CONTENT

Melodic
    New Notes on the 5th String: A, B, and C
    Songs:
        "The House of the Rising Sun"
        "5th String Boogie"

Chordal
    Key of A Minor: Am, Dm, and E7 Chords
    New Time Signature: 6/8
    Fingerpicking Pattern 4
    Song: "Blue Minor"

Theory
    Chord Construction
    Major Chord Construction Worksheet
    Ear Training
    Minor Chord Construction Worksheet
    Song:
        "The House of the Rising Sun" (strum part)

Stylistic
    Classical Music and the Guitar
    The Modern Classical Guitar
    Song: "Aguado Study in A Minor"
    Artist Portrait: Andrés Segovia
    Song: "Giuliani Study in A Minor"

NEW VOCABULARY

interval: The distance between two notes. Intervals are measured in steps.

major 3rd interval: Two whole steps

minor 3rd interval: A whole step plus a half step

relative major and relative minor: Major and minor keys that share the same key signature

syncopation: Rhythm with emphasis or stress on a weak beat or weak portion of a beat

The Notes on the 5th String

New Notes: A, B, and C CD 2:2

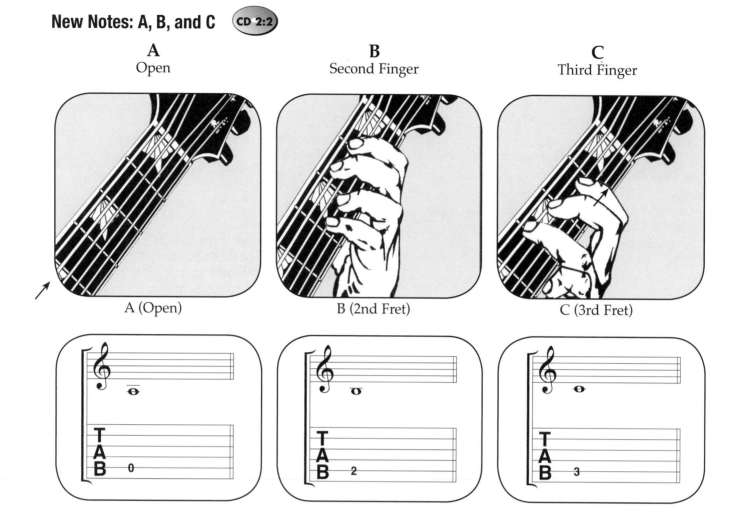

A
Open

B
Second Finger

C
Third Finger

A (Open)

B (2nd Fret)

C (3rd Fret)

Example 1

Example 2: Use strict alternate picking on the eighth notes. This example introduces the A minor scale. You'll learn more about the A minor scale and the key of A minor in the next few lessons.

Example 3

"The House of the Rising Sun" is a traditional folk song. Eric Burden and the Animals had a hit with their blues/rock version in the mid-1960s.

The House of the Rising Sun CD 2:3

Traditional

There is a house in New Or - leans, they call the
tell my ba - by sis - ter, now, don't do what

Ris - ing Sun._____ It's been the ruin of man - y poor
I have done;_____ but shun the house in New____ Or -

girls, and I, oh Lord, am one._____ Go
leans, they call the Ris - in' Sun._____

"5th-String Boogie" takes the basic rock bass-line riff you learned on page 60 and expands on it once again, this time in the context of a blues in A. You will learn more about the key of A and blues chord progressions later. Note the following:

- Use strict down-up picking as indicated.

- Notice the syncopation on the last note of every other measure (on the "and" of beat 4).
  Syncopation—Rhythm with the emphasis or stress on a weak beat or weak portion of a beat.

- This arrangement use three accidentals: C♯ on the 5th string/4th fret; F♯ on the 4th string/4th fret; and G♯ on the 3rd string/1st fret. Use the indicated left-hand fingerings.

- Just as you did in "Rock Riffs in D" on page 60, play these riffs in 2nd position (first finger at the 2nd fret) except measures 9 and 10, which return to 1st position.

- For the ending, simply repeat the two-bar riff over and over, getting softer each time.

5th-String Boogie (2nd position) CD 2:4

The keys of C major and A minor contain the same notes and share the same key signature (no sharps or flats). Therefore, these two keys are referred to as **major and relative minor.**

The relative minor scale always starts on the sixth note of its relative major scale. The following diagram shows how the C major scale and the A minor scale overlap each other. You can see that the A minor scale is the same as a C major scale beginning and ending on the sixth note. (You actually played an A minor scale in Examples 2 and 3 on page 64.)

Even though C major and A minor share the same key signature, there are some obvious differences.

Songs in C major:

- tend to center around the note C,
- usually begin and end on a C chord (the **I** chord in C),
- use the G7 chord (the **V7** in C), which the ear hears as wanting to resolve (return) to C, and
- have the consonant, uplifting sound associated with major keys.

Songs in A minor:

- tend to center around the note A,
- usually begin and end on an A minor chord (the **I** chord in A minor),
- use the E7 chord (the **V7** in A minor), which the ear hears as wanting to resolve (return) to A, and
- have the melancholy sound associated with minor keys.

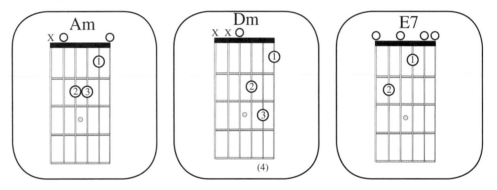

To play the Am chord:
- Place your second finger on the 4th string, just behind the 2nd fret.
- Place your third finger on the 3rd string, just behind the 2nd fret.
- Place your first finger on the 2nd string, just behind the 1st fret.
- The 5th and 1st strings are played open.

To play the Dm chord:
- Place your second finger on the 3rd string, just behind the 2nd fret.
- Place your third (or 4th) finger on the 2nd string, just behind the 3rd fret.
- Place your first finger on the 1st string, just behind the 1st fret.
- The 4th string is played open.

To play the E7 chord:
- Place your second finger on the 5th string, just behind the 2nd fret.
- Place your first finger on the 3rd string, just behind the 1st fret.
- The 5th, 2nd, and 1st strings are played open.

Practice each chord. Strum through the chord and try to get a clear sound with all the notes ringing.

This next song uses the Am, Dm, and E7 chords. It can easily be played with a pick or fingerstyle.

- To play it with a pick, use all downstrokes.
- To play it fingerstyle, use Fingerpicking Pattern 4: p i m a m i (Notice the pattern: thumb–index–middle–ring–middle–index, and repeat.)
- Notice the classic melancholy minor sound.

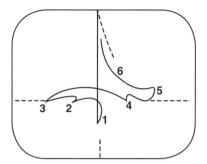

$\frac{6}{8}$ conducting pattern:

New Time Signature:

$\mathbf{6}$ = six beats per measure
$\mathbf{8}$ = an eighth note gets one beat

Listen to the recording to get the feel of the rhythm.

Think of the rhythm as two groups of three beats:

6/8:	1 2 3	4 5 6
Fingerpicking Pattern 4:	p i m	a m i

Example 1: Fingerpicking Pattern 4

"Blue Minor" can be played with a pick or using the previous fingerpicking pattern. Tab is included to help you find the fingerings.

Dotted quarter note (♩.) = three eighth notes. The song ends with a dotted quarter note. A dotted quarter note is equal to three eighth notes, so in 6/8 time it receives three beats. Let all the notes ring throughout each measure.

Blue Minor CD 2:7

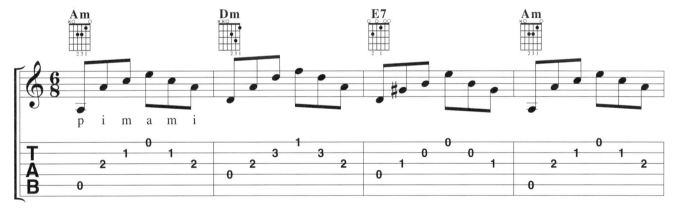

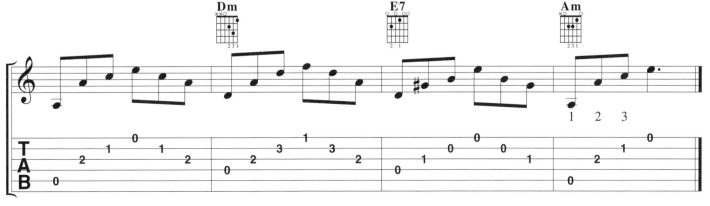

Ear Training CD 2:8

Until now you have been singing scale passages in major keys. As you learned on page 66, the A minor scale begins on the 6th degree of the C major scale. So, to sing a minor scale, you will use the solfège syllables starting on "la."

Example 1

La   Ti   Do   Ti   La

Example 2

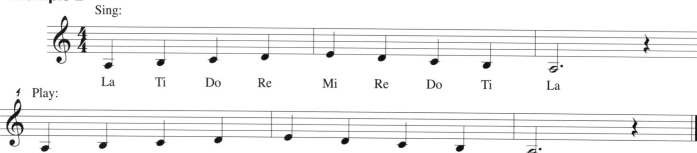

La   Ti   Do   Re   Mi   Re   Do   Ti   La

Intervals and Chord Construction

An **interval** is a measurement of the distance between two notes.

Major 3rd Interval: A major 3rd (maj3rd) is equal to two whole steps (2).

Minor 3rd Interval: A minor 3rd (min3rd) is equal to a whole step plus a half step (1 1/2).

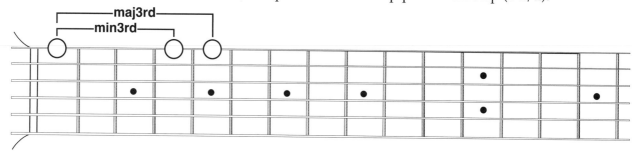

1. Using the C major scale as a reference, determine the interval between each of the followng pairs of notes and then fill in the following blanks (the first one is done for you):

	C		D		E		F		G		A		B		C
		1		1		1/2		1		1		1		1/2	

C to E: <u>maj3rd (1 + 1)</u>   G to B: _____

D to F: _____   A to C: _____

E to G: _____   B to D: _____

F to A: _____

2. In the key of C what are the notes in the **IV** chord?   ____   ____   ____
    Fill in the intervals between these notes.   ____   ____

    In the key of C what are the notes in the **IV** chord?   ____   ____   ____
    Fill in the intervals between these notes.   ____   ____

    In the key of C what are the notes in the **V** chord?   ____   ____   ____
    Fill in the intervals between these notes.   ____   ____

    In the key of C what are the notes in the **V7** chord?   ____   ____   ____   ____
    Fill in the intervals between these notes.   ____   ____   ____

If you've filled in the proceeding correctly, you will see that major chords are constructed from a maj3rd + min3rd, and dominant 7th chords are constructed from a maj3rd + min3rd + min3rd.

Following is an A minor scale. The whole steps and half steps are indicated. To review: **All adjacent natural notes are one whole step apart, except E–F and B–C, which are natural half steps** (review page 54).

A Minor Scale:

A		B		C		D		E		F		G		A
	1		1/2		1		1		1/2		1			1

Minor Chord Construction: As you learned on the previous page, major chords are constructed from a major 3rd (two whole steps) plus a minor 3rd (1 1/2 steps). Minor chords are the exact opposite. **Therefore, a minor chord is constructed from a minor 3rd plus a major 3rd.**

Using the A minor scale shown above, fill in the following:

What are the notes in the **I** chord?   ___ ___ ___   Is this chord major or minor? _____

What are the notes in the **IV** chord? ___ ___ ___   Is this chord major or minor? _____

What are the notes in the **V** chord?   ___ ___ ___   Is this chord major or minor? _____

Often the chords in a minor key song are based on the **harmonic minor scale** instead of the "pure" minor scale that is shown above. In a harmonic minor scale the 7th note is raised one half-step; so there is one note difference between the two scales. Notice the "G" has been raised to "G♯."

A Harmonic Minor Scale:

A		B		C		D		E		F		G♯		A
	1		1/2		1		1		1/2		1 1/2			1/2

Using the A harmonic minor scale, fill in the following:

What are the notes in the **I** chord?   ___ ___ ___   Is this chord major or minor? _____

What are the notes in the **IV** chord? ___ ___ ___   Is this chord major or minor? _____

What are the notes in the **V** chord?   ___ ___ ___   Is this chord major or minor ? _____

What are the notes in the **V7** chord?   ___ ___ ___ ___   Is this chord major, minor, or major or dom7? _____

Review:

Major chords = maj3rd + min3rd

Minor chords = min3rd + maj3rd

Dominant 7th chords = maj3rd + min3rd + min3rd

About Classical Guitar

The modern guitar evolved from early stringed folk instruments such as the lute, but guitar-like instruments were common in virtually all early cultures from Europe and throughout Asia. The classical guitar traces its roots to eighteenth- and nineteenth-century Europe and Spain. Early composers for the guitar include Fernando Sor (1778–1839) and Dionysio Aguado (1784–1849), both of Spain, and Matteo Carcassi (1792–1853), Ferdinando Carulli (1770–1841), and Mauro Giuliani (1781–1829) of Italy. In the early nineteenth century the guitar began to gain enormous popularity, especially among amateur and folk musicians due to the ease with which it could be used to create simple yet highly effective and beautiful song accompaniments. However, during this period, relatively few performers attempted to master the complexities of guitar technique required to perform the small but growing body of guitar masterworks being composed. Very few of the great classical performers and composers considered the guitar a serious instrument due to the small number of virtuoso performers and also because the soft, relatively quiet sound produced by early guitars limited those instruments to intimate parlor performances—the guitar could not be heard above most other instruments in most ensembles let alone above the sound of a symphony orchestra. Not until Andrés Segovia gained popularity did the guitar begin to be taken seriously as a concert instrument.

About the Modern Classical Guitar

The modern classical guitar is a highly refined successor to its nineteenth-century counterparts. Spanish guitar builder Antonio de Torres (1817–1892) is credited with refining the design upon which all modern classical guitars are based. The classical guitar is larger than its predecessors and, thanks to Torres's perfected construction techniques, much louder. The typical classical guitar is similar in appearance to the flamenco guitar discussed previously. However, the back and sides are made of rosewood, and the top is usually spruce or cedar; plus, the strings are set higher above the neck, giving the classical guitar a much richer, darker tone than the very bright flamenco instrument.

Aguado Study: Here is a piece written by Dionysio Aguado. As with most classical guitar music, it is meant to be played fingerstyle, not with a pick.

- The piece is in A minor (note the chord progression).

- All the notes with down-stems are played with your thumb. These are half notes and should ring for two full beats—while you play the up-stemmed eighth notes with your fingers.

- This piece is played by arpeggiating the indicated partial chord fingerings (an arpeggio is a chord played one note at a time). Use the fingering indicated in the chord diagrams.

- Classical improvisation: Have a second guitarist improvise a strummed or fingerpicked accompaniment based on the standard Am, E7, A7, and Dm chord fingerings.

Aguado Study in A Minor

70

Artist Portrait: Andrés Segovia
(1893–1987)

© Hulton-Deutsch Collection//CORBIS

Andrés Segovia grew up in Granada, Spain, an area rich in the tradition of flamenco. Early on he made it his mission to establish the guitar as a serious concert instrument on the world stage. He recognized the lack of substantial repertoire for the instrument and set about transcribing the works of great Spanish and European composers for guitar. In addition, as he revealed the potential of the instrument, many leading composers began composing new music specifically for guitar. The repertoire that Segovia established has become the standard repertoire for which the classical guitar is best known.

Giuliani Study: Like the previous piece, this classical guitar study is in A minor. The original version of this piece was written for solo fingerstyle guitar. This arrangement is a duet, and both parts should be played with a pick.

- The chord progression is indicated throughout. Each chord is held for two complete measures.

- Every measure begins on the "and" of 1 with an up-stroke. Count to yourself, say "1," and then play the first note with an up-stroke on the "and" of 1.

- Some interesting chords are created by changing one note. For example:

  - In bar 11 drop the C down to B in the Am chord. B is the 2nd note of an A minor scale, so this forms an A(2) chord.

  - In bar 12 lower the A to G♯. This creates an E chord that is being played above an A bass note, so the chord symbol is E/A.

Giuliani Study in A Minor (Duet) CD 2:12

The Blues
Blues music developed in the early 1900s from field hollers (music sung in the cotton fields), early spirituals, and Gospel music performed in rural southern black churches.

NEW CONTENT

Melodic
    New Notes on the 6th String: E, F, and G
    Songs:
        "Spanish Serenade"
        "Surf-Rock Bass"

Chordal
    Key of E Minor: Em, Am, B7 Chords
    "Surf-Rock Bass" Accompaniment

Theory
    Key of E Minor
    Ear Training
    Chord Construction Worksheet
    Fingerpicking Pattern 5
    Song: "Rock Ballad"

Stylistic
    The Blues
    Artist Portrait: Blind Boy Fuller
    Song: "E Minor Blues"

The Notes on the 6th String

New Notes: E, F, and G

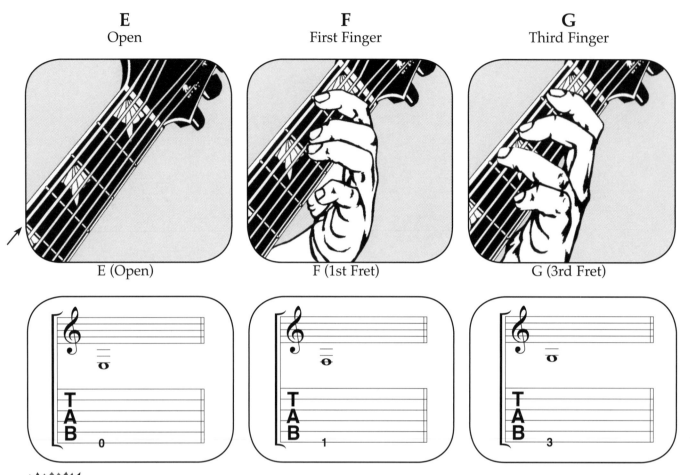

> **Note** The notes on the 6th string are the same as the notes on the 1st string, only two octaves lower.

Example 1

Example 2

Example 3

"Spanish Serenade" is based on a common flamenco chord progression: Am–G–F–E. Once you can play this song as a solo, try improvising a strum-style accompaniment using the indicated chords.

New Chord

To play an F chord lay your first finger flat across the 1st and 2nd strings at the 1st fret. Then place your 2nd and 3rd fingers as shown.

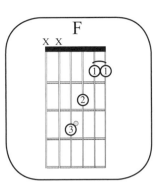

Spanish Serenade (Duet) CD 2:14

You've heard variations on this next guitar part many times, especially in the music of early surf and rocka-billy guitarists like the Ventures, Dick Dale, and Duane Eddy. To get a really authentic sound, use an electric guitar on the lead pickup with lots of reverb.

Notice the key signature—one sharp (F#). This song is in the key of E minor. Just as the key of A minor has the same key signature as C major, the key of E minor has the same key signature as G major.

Surf-Rock Bass CD 2:15

The keys of G major and E minor contain the same notes and have the same key signature. Therefore, these two keys are **major and relative minor,** just as A minor is the relative minor of C major.

Review: The relative minor scale always starts on the sixth note of its relative major scale. You can see that the E minor scale is the same as a G major scale beginning and ending on the sixth note.

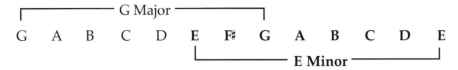

Songs in G major:

- tend to center around the note G,
- usually begin and end on a G chord (the **I** chord in G),
- use the D7 chord (the **V7** in G), which the ear hears as wanting to resolve (return) to G, and
- have the consonant, uplifting sound associated with major keys.

Songs in E minor:

- tend to center around the note E,
- usually begin and end on an E minor chord (the **I** chord in E minor),
- use the B7 chord (the **V7** in E minor), which the ear hears as wanting to resolve (return) to E, and
- have the melancholy sound associated with minor keys.

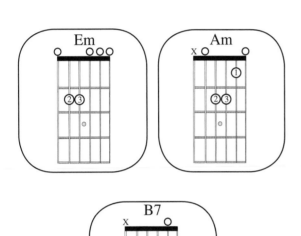

You've already learned the A minor chord.

To play the Em chord:
- Place your second finger on the 5th string, just behind the 2nd fret.
- Place your third finger on the 4th string, just behind the 2nd fret.
- The 6th, 3rd, 2nd and 1st strings are played open.

To play the B7 chord:
- Place your second finger on the 5th string, just behind the 2nd fret.
- Place your first finger on the 4th string, just behind the 1st.
- Place your third finger on the 3rd string, just behind the 2nd fret.
- Place your fourth finger on the 1st string, just behind the 2nd fret.
- The 2nd string is played open.

Here is the accompaniment part for "Surf-Rock Bass." Use it to practice your Em, Am, and B7 chords. The rake symbol (≹) indicates to brush your pick through the strings, creating a harp-like sound.

Surf-Rock (Accompaniment) CD 2:17

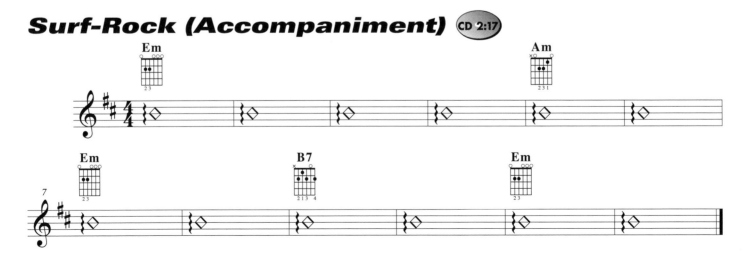

Ear Training

Example 1

La   Ti   Do   Ti   La

Example 2

La   Ti   Do   Re   Mi   Re   Do   Ti   La

Chord Construction Review

Major chords are constructed from a major 3rd (two whole steps) plus a minor 3rd (1 1/2 steps).

Minor chords are constructed from a minor 3rd plus a major 3rd.

Dominant 7th chords are constructed from a maj3rd plus a min3rd plus a min3rd.

Here is an E "pure" minor scale. Fill in the whole steps and half steps. (Remember: All adjacent natural notes are one whole step apart, except E–F and B–C, which are natural half steps.)

E   F♯   G   A   B   C   D   E

____   ____   ____   ____   ____   ____   ____

Using the E minor scale, fill in the following blanks. Remember, you can always figure out the notes in the **I, IV,** and **V** chords by starting on the root of each chord and then counting up to the 3rd and 5th notes from the root (every other note). Make sure to count the root as "1."

What are the notes in the **I** chord?   ___ ___ ___   Is this chord major or minor? _____

What are the notes in the **IV** chord?   ___ ___ ___   Is this chord major or minor? _____

What are the notes in the **V** chord?   ___ ___ ___   Is this chord major or minor? _____

As you learned previously, the chords in a minor key song are often based on the harmonic minor scale instead of the pure minor scale. Here is the E harmonic minor scale (notice the 7th note has been raised one half step). Fill in the whole steps and half steps. (Remember, in the harmonic minor scale there is one interval of 1 and 1/2 steps.)

E Harmonic Minor Scale:

E   F♯   G   A   B   C   D♯   E

____   ____   ____   ____   ____   ____   ____

Using the E harmonic minor scale, fill in the following blanks:

What are the notes in the **I** chord?   ___ ___ ___   Is this chord major or minor? _____

What are the notes in the **IV** chord?   ___ ___ ___   Is this chord major or minor? _____

What are the notes in the **V** chord?   ___ ___ ___   Is this chord major or minor? _____

What are the notes in the **V7** chord?   ___ ___ ___ ___   Is this chord major, minor, or dom7? _____

Now you'll learn a common fingerpicking pattern that will work well for accompaniments in 4/4 time. Practice the following example slowly and carefully until you can play it with a steady, uninterrupted rhythm. For this exercise you'll use a G and an E minor chord, but any fingerpicking pattern can be applied to any chord.

Fingerpicking Pattern 5: p i m i a i m i

- Hold the G chord.
- Plant your right-hand thumb (p) on the bass note, 6th string.
- Plant your right-hand index finger (i) on the 3rd string.
- Plant your right-hand middle finger (m) on the 2nd string.
- Plant your right-hand third finger (a) on the 1st string.
- **Notice that every other note is played by the index finger.**

Now practice Example 1 until you can play it smoothly, without stopping.

Example 1: Fingerpicking Pattern 5 CD 2:19

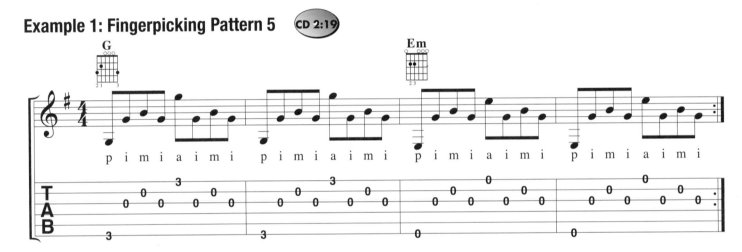

Now you are ready to learn both parts to "Rock Ballad":

- Guitar 1 is a pick-style part that alternates between chord arpeggios and strumming. Hold the indicated chord for each measure.
- Guitar 2 uses Fingerpicking Pattern 5 throughout. Once you memorize the pattern, apply it to every chord.
- Guitar 2 is indicated in notation, tab, and with chord grids so that you can see that although the part may look complicated, it is actually simple and repetitive.
- This song introduces the low F♯ at the 2nd fret on the 6th string.

Rock Ballad (Duet) CD 2:20

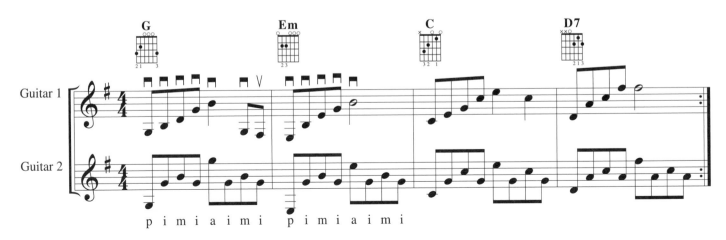

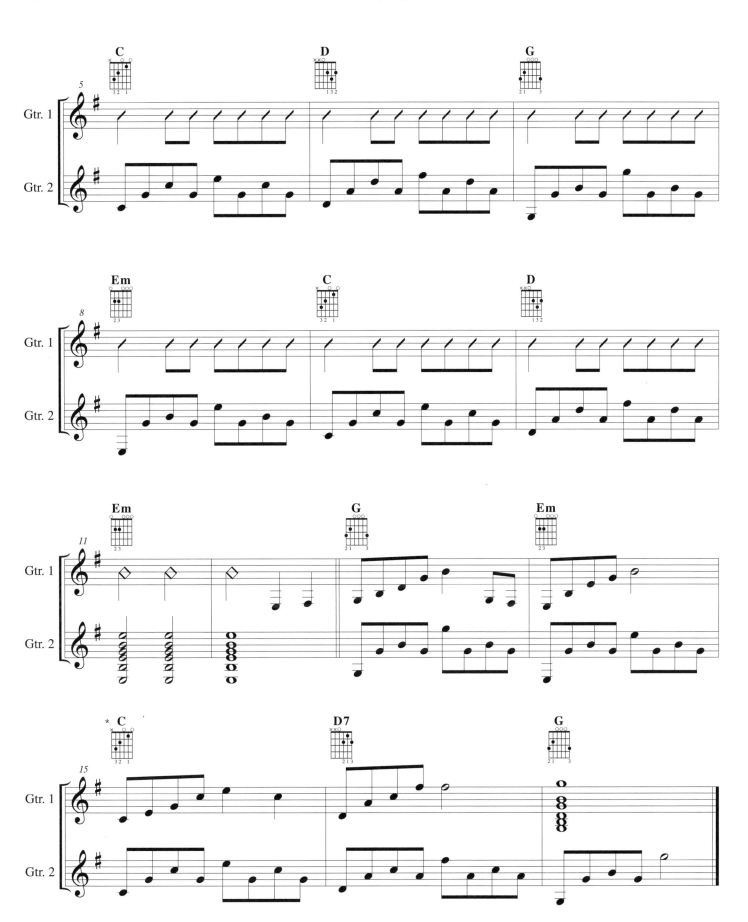

*Brush through the chord with your thumb.

About the Blues

Blues music developed in the early 1900s from field hollers (music sung in the cotton fields), early spirituals, and gospel music performed in rural southern black churches. Blues was the music that was performed at black social functions such as parties, dances, and roadhouses. Often the blues was performed in secret, since the local churches usually forbade their members to perform secular, or nonreligious, music.

Modern blues has evolved from many sources and regions. The two primary sources of influence on modern blues are:

- The early rural acoustic blues music of the 1920s and '30s, mostly from rural southern regions such as the Mississippi Delta and North Carolina. Early rural blues artists include Robert Johnson and Charley Patton, both of the Delta region, and Blind Boy Fuller and Rev. Gary Davis, both from the North Carolina area. Typically this kind of blues is performed by a solo guitarist/singer and an acoustic guitar, fingerstyle.

- The more sophisticated electric urban blues of the 1940s. Early electric blues artists include Muddy Waters (McKinley Morganfield), Howlin' Wolf, T. Bone Walker, and B.B. King, who came along a little later. This style of blues was centered around Chicago and was usually performed on electric guitar with a full band.

Blues has evolved since its early beginnings and has influenced many modern styles of music, especially jazz and rock. Listen to Blind Boy Fuller's recording of "Corinne, What Makes You Treat Me So?" This example of early rural blues was recorded in 1934.

The Blues Form: Most blues songs follow a basic three-chord (**I**, **IV**, and **V**), 12-measure form ("Corinne" is a 16-measure form). Usually the form is broken into three phrases: phrase 1 is four measures, phrase 2 is usually a repeat of phrase 1 but with different chords (**IV** and **I**), and then phrase 3 is an answer to the first two phrases. Can you identify the three phrases as you listen to "Corinne, What Makes You Treat Me So?"?

Artist Portrait: Fulton Allen (Blind Boy Fuller)

Fulton Allen was born in Durham, North Carolina, in 1907 and died in 1941. He was a laborer in a coal yard when he began to lose his sight in his late teens. Once he lost his sight, Fulton "Blind Boy Fuller" Allen was forced to play and sing on street corners to make a living during the height of the Great Depression in the early 1930s. He began by teaching himself to play. He also studied with the great Reverend Gary Davis, and together they are credited with defining the style of early rural blues music that grew out of rural Carolina (known as the Piedmont style). In 1934, while performing on a street corner, Blind Boy Fuller was discovered by a young record store owner and blues fan, James Baxter Long. Mr. Long brought Blind Boy and Gary Davis to New York for their first recording sessions.

Photo Courtesy of Stephen Grossman

The Blues Guitar

Any type of guitar can and has been used to perform the blues. Many blues artists played inexpensive (or even home-made) acoustic guitars since they couldn't usually afford the high-priced models. However, some of the guitar types that are most often associated with the blues are:

- Small-bodied acoustic guitars like the Gibson L-00™. The small bodies and wide necks on these guitars make them well suited for fingerstyle solo acoustic blues.

- Semi-hollow-body electric guitars like the Gibson Lucille™ (B.B. King's signature guitar, based on the Gibson 335 model) are popular with Chicago-style electric blues artists.

- Resonator guitars have a metal cone that produces a bright and loud sound that is often associated with the blues. These guitars are often played with a slide as well as with a pick or fingers.

Gibson L-00™

Gibson Lucille™

Resonator

"E Minor Blues" is based on the chord progression to B.B. King's classic song "The Thrill Is Gone."

- This is an arpeggio-style accompaniment part based on the **I, IV,** and **V** chords in the key of E minor (plus a C chord).

- The fingerpicking pattern for this song is based on Fingerpicking Pattern 5 with one important difference: Notice how an interesting bass line is created by using your thumb on the "and" of beat 4 instead of your index finger (measures 2, 4, 6, etc.).

- Let each of the notes ring, especially the bass note on beat 1 of each measure. This note should continue to ring for the full measure.

E Minor Blues CD 2:23

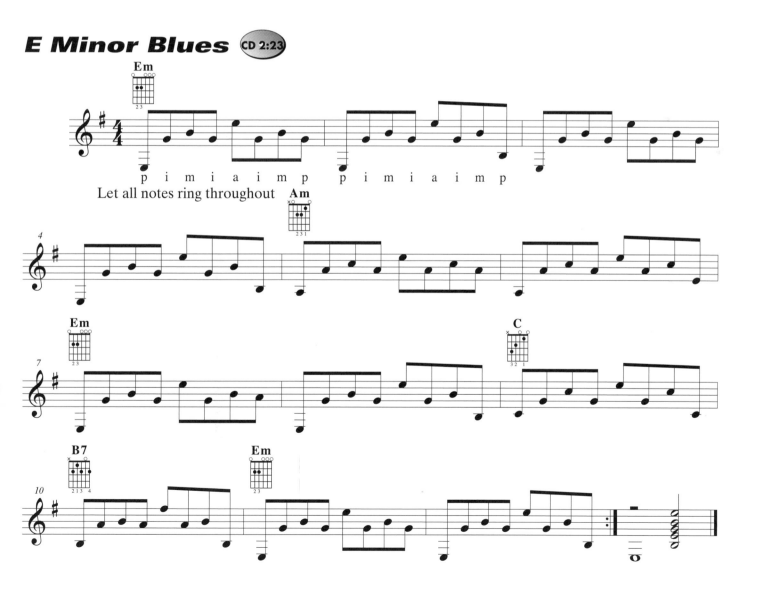

Blues-Rock Guitar

In the mid-sixties some rock artists began to get very serious about exploring the blues roots of rock-and-roll. In fact, many of the early recordings by Eric Clapton, Led Zeppelin, the Rolling Stones, and even the Beatles were actually "covers" (new versions) of hits from their favorite blues artists.

NEW CONTENT

Theory
    Major Scale Construction (Review)
    Ear Training
    "A Major Etude"

Chordal
    Key of A: A, D, E, and E7 Chords
    Strum Pattern 4 (Alternating Bass)
    Songs:
        "Wild Thing" Pattern
        "Twist and Shout" Pattern

Stylistic
    Blues-Rock
    The Blues Song Form
    The Blues Boogie Pattern
    Boogie Example 1
    Song: "Blue Boogie in A"
    Blues Soloing
    Minor Pentatonic Scale
    Improvising a Blues Solo
    New Phrasing Techniques: Vibrato,
        Hammer-on, Pull-off, and String Bends

Review and Practice
    Key of A Minor
    Song: "Für Elise"

Review and Practice
    Song: "A Boogie Blues"

NEW VOCABULARY

1st position: Left hand is placed so that the first finger is at the 1st fret, the second finger at the 2nd fret, etc.

2nd position: Left hand is placed so that the first finger is at the second fret, the second finger at the 3rd fret, etc.

improvise: To create and perform music, speech, or movement on the spot

power chord: A common slang term for two-note chords consisting of just the root and the 5th (no 3rd)

shuffle feel: A term used in rock and blues to refer to an uneven eighth-note feel; similar to swing feel

Major Scale Construction (Review)

Half Step: A half step (1/2) is the distance from a note to the next closest note (C to C♯, C♯ to D, D to D♯, etc.). This is the same as the distance from one fret to the next.

Whole Step: A whole step (1) is equal to two half steps. So, this is the same as a two-fret distance.

Major Scale

As you learned on page 54, major scales are constructed from the following pattern of whole steps and half steps:

1 1 1/2 1 1 1 1/2

Remember: All adjacent natural (not sharp or flat) notes are a whole step apart (1), except E–F and B–C, which are both natural half steps (1/2).

Below are the notes from A to A. Fill in the required pattern of whole and half steps below the notes and then fill in the appropriate sharp signs for the A major scale.

A   B   C   D   E   F   G   A

___ ___ ___ ___ ___ ___ ___ ___

Below is a blank fretboard diagram. Draw an A major scale from open A on just the 5th string. After you draw the scale, play it with one finger.

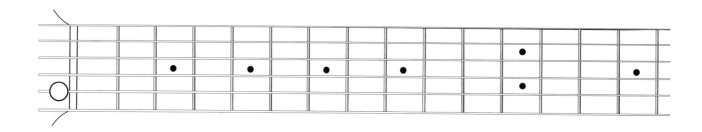

Ear Training CD 2:24

Sing and play the A major scale (sing in the octave most comfortable for you).

Notice the key signature: Three sharps (F♯, C♯, and G♯) is A major.

Example 1

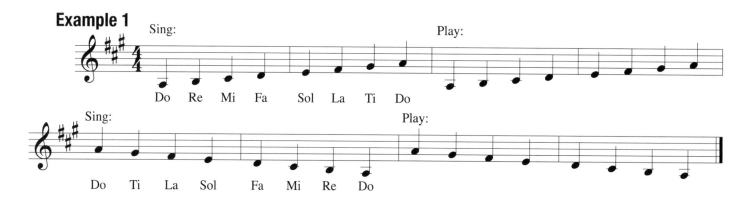

Sing: Do Re Mi Fa Sol La Ti Do   Play:

Sing: Do Ti La Sol Fa Mi Re Do   Play:

The A Major Scale CD 2:25

Until now, most of the melodies you have played are in 1st position, meaning that the first finger of your left hand was anchored at the 1st fret. The following fingering for the A major scale moves from the 1st position to the 2nd position (first finger at the 2nd fret). Practice this fingering for the A major scale until you can play it comfortably from memory.

Notice that in this fingering, instead of playing B on the open 2nd string, you play it at the 4th fret on the 3rd string, and instead of playing E on the open 1st string, you play it at the 5th fret on the 2nd string.

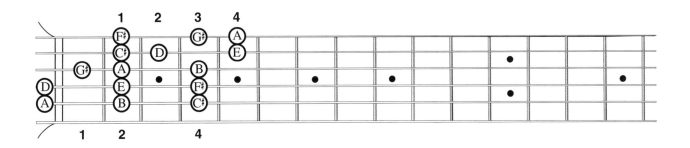

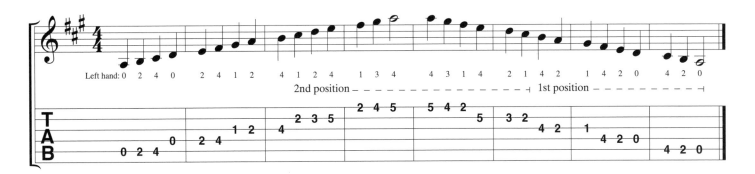

Now try "A Major Etude" based on the A major scale fingering.

A Major Etude CD 2:26

CD 2:27

Following is an A major scale. As you can see, in the key of A, A is the **I** chord, D is the **IV** chord, E is the **V** chord, and E7 is the **V7** chord.

A	B	C#	D	E	F#	G#	A
I	II	III	IV	V	VI	VII	VIII

In previous sections, you learned the A, D, and E7 chords. Here they are again, plus the E major chord, for review.

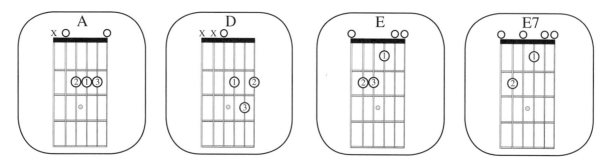

Strum through each chord and try to get a clear sound with all the notes ringing. Make sure the notes are not being accidentally muted by nearby fingers.

"Strum Pattern 4" introduces the alternating bass style of accompaniment. This style is very common, especially in fast country and bluegrass music:

1. On beat 1 play the bass note of the chord (the root).

2. On beat 2 strum the rest of the chord (do not play the bass note again).

3. On beat 3 play the alternate bass note (usually the 5th of the chord).

4. On beat 4 strum the rest of the chord (again, do not repeat the bass note).

Example 1: Strum Pattern 4 – Alternating Bass CD 2:28

SECTION 8 • Key of A: I, IV, and V7 Chords

Previously you learned several three-chord rock-and-roll guitar parts in G and D. Here they are again, only this time in the key of A. The more you apply these kinds of strum patterns to different keys, the easier it gets.

Below is the "Wild Thing" rhythm pattern. Use all down-strokes for the strum.

The "Wild Thing" Pattern CD 2:29

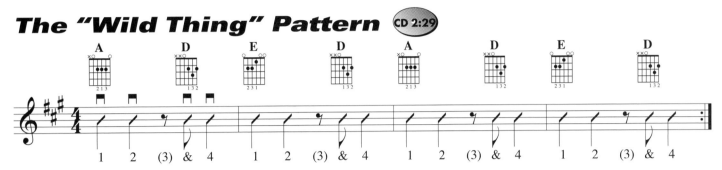

Below is the "Twist and Shout" rhythm pattern. Use down- and up-strokes as indicated. Notice the rest on beat 4. Just keep a constant down-up strumming motion and "miss" the strings (a down-stroke) on beat 4, which puts you in position to play the E chord with an up-stroke on the "and" of 4.

The "Twist and Shout" Pattern CD 2:30

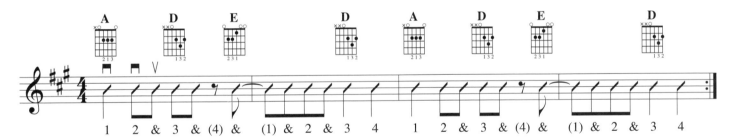

About Blues-Rock

In the mid-sixties some rock artists began to get serious about exploring the blues roots of rock-and-roll. In fact, many of the early recordings by Eric Clapton, Led Zeppelin, the Rolling Stones, and even the Beatles were actually covers (new versions) of hits from their favorite blues artists, such as Muddy Waters, Buddy Guy, and Willie Dixon. Blues-rock remains one of the most important genres of rock music. Some more recent blues-rock artists include ZZ Top, Stevie Ray Vaughan, Jonny Lang, and Kenny Wayne Shepherd.

The Blues Song Form: Previously you learned about the blues as a specific style or genre. But now you will take a look at the musical form of the blues. The blues is the most common song form in popular music. The basic blues chord progression is 12 measures (bars) long and is built on the **I, IV,** and **V** chords. Here is the basic standard blues form:

Can you find the blues progressions on pages 65, 75, and 81? What, if any, are the differences between the blues progressions on those pages and the progression shown above?

The Blues Boogie Pattern

The blues boogie pattern and its countless variations comprise the backbone of rock-and-roll and blues rhythm guitar styles. The basic boogie pattern is based on alternating between two simple two-note chords: a power 5th chord (root and 5th) and a two-note 6th chord (root and 6th).

Power Chord: A common slang term for two-note chords consisting of just the root and the 5th (no 3rd). These chords function like big bass notes and produce a very big, powerful bass-line–driven sound.

The key of A is the most common key for guitar boogie progressions. Below are the chords for a key-of-A blues boogie progression.

Note:

- Each chord uses an open-string bass note.
- The upper note of the power 5 chord is played with your first finger.
- Do not lift your first finger off the string when placing your third finger down to play the 6th chord.

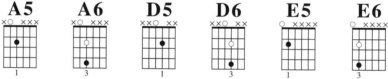

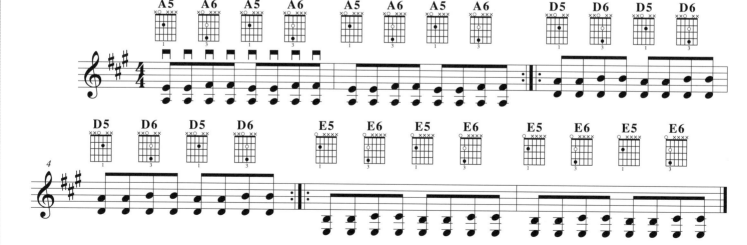

Below is a basic key-of-A boogie progression. Practice it with a straight eighth-note feel and a swing eighth-note feel. Note that **in blues and rock, a swing eighth feel (uneven eighths) is called a shuffle feel.**

Note:
- Remember, this type of pattern is usually played with all down-strokes. Down-strokes provide a more driving rhythmic feel than down-up strokes.

- Play this progression with both a straight eighth and a shuffle (uneven) eighth feel. Typically, shuffle grooves are more common in blues and are usually slower than straight eighth grooves, which are more common in rock-and-roll.

- Try using a right-hand palm mute for a more authentic rock and blues feel. To play a palm mute, gently rest the palm of your picking hand against the strings just above the bridge. This technique should mute the strings, producing a driving percussive feel. Listen to the recorded example.

- This pattern is a variation on "Boogie Example 1."

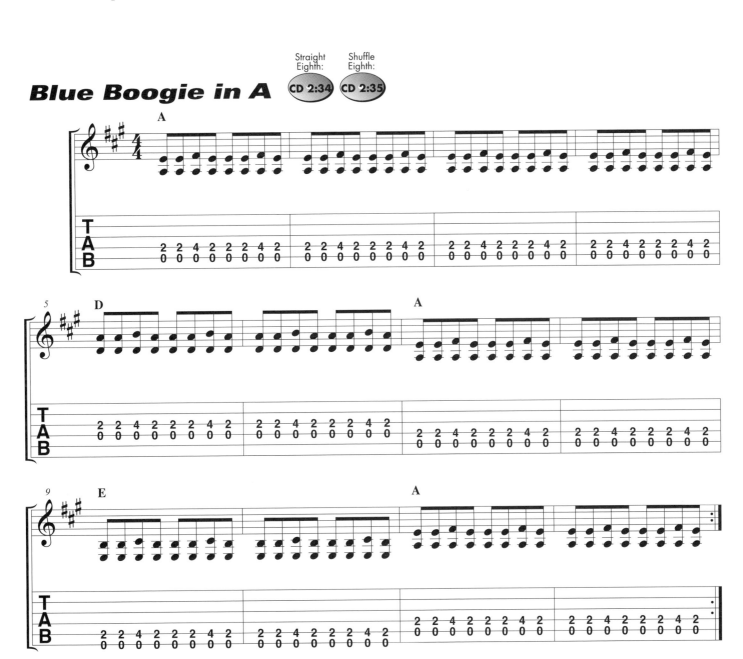

Blue Boogie in A

Straight Eighth: CD 2:34 Shuffle Eighth: CD 2:35

About "Für Elise"

Below is a guitar duet based on one of Beethoven's most popular pieces, "Für Elise." Although originally written for solo piano, this classical piece has been arranged for many different instruments in solo and ensemble formats. Learn both parts and play each one along with the included recording.

Guitar 1:

- The song is in A minor.
- Use your fourth finger for the 2nd string D#.

Guitar 2:

- The accompaniment part is built from standard guitar chords in the key of A minor (another example of how even classical music can be broken down into basic chord progressions).
- The G/B in measure 12 is a partial voicing of the basic G chord (the middle four strings).

Für Elise CD 2:36

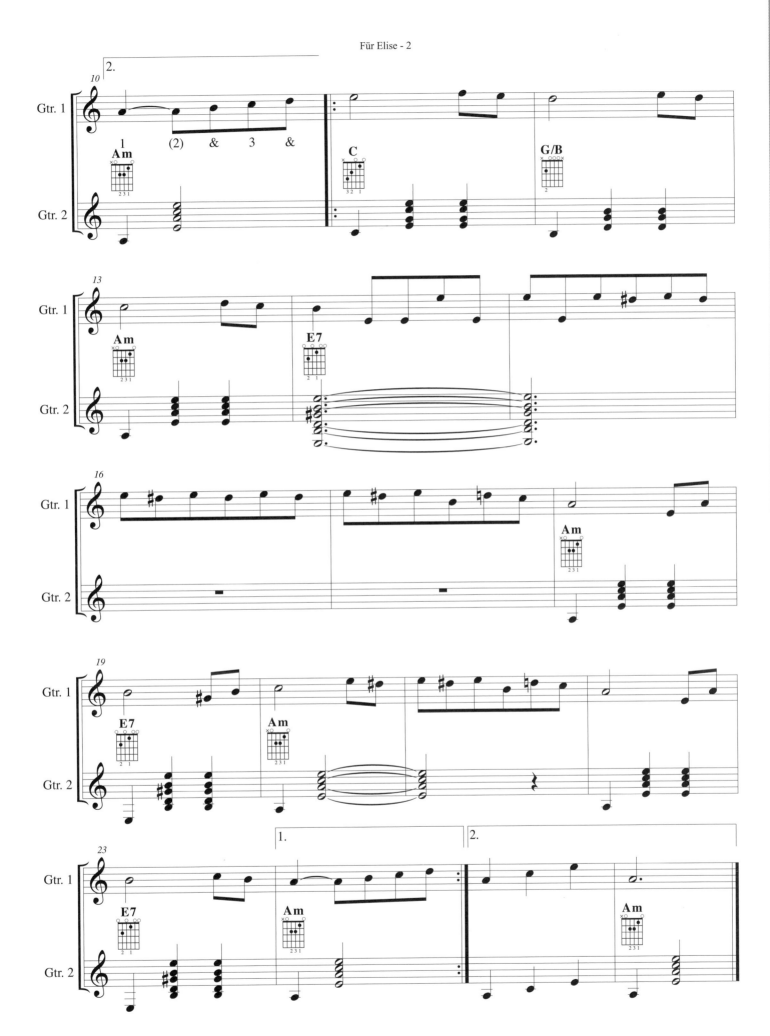

On page 88 you learned about the basic blues progression and the basic guitar boogie pattern. This next example is a variation on the "Blue Boogie in A" that you learned on page 89 and on the bass-line boogie patterns you learned on pages 60 and 65. As always, learn both parts, play each along with the recording or with a friend.

Guitar 1

- This guitar part consists of a straightforward strumming pattern using the full chord forms.

- Notice the change from A to A7 in measure 4.

- Use down-up strumming.

Guitar 2

- This pattern combines the boogie bass-line riff with the two-note boogie chord pattern.

- Use all down-strokes. (At faster tempos switch to down-up.)

- Use a right-hand palm mute: Slightly mute (muffle) the strings by gently resting the palm of your picking hand against the strings just above the bridge.

- Practice the song with both a straight eighth note feel (demonstrated on CD 2, Track 37) and with a shuffle feel (demonstrated on CD 2, Track 38).

A Boogie Blues

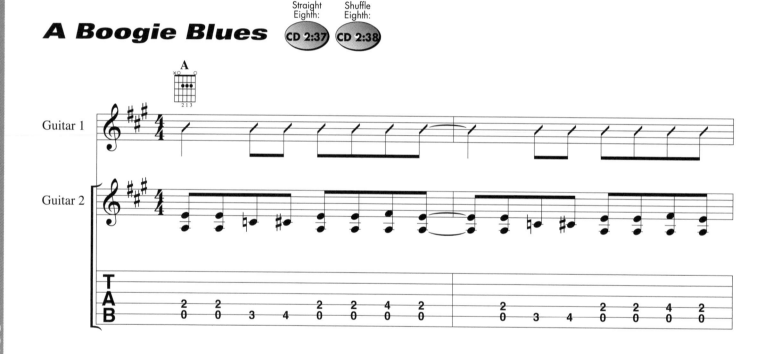

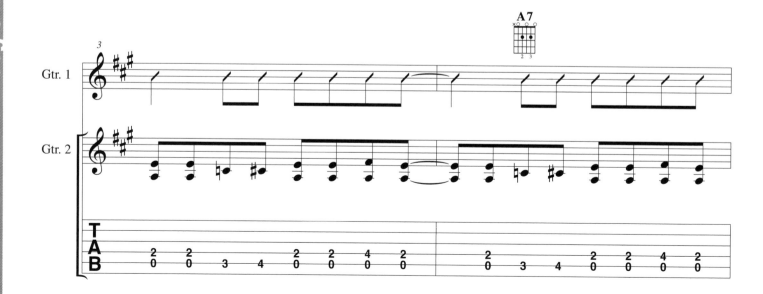

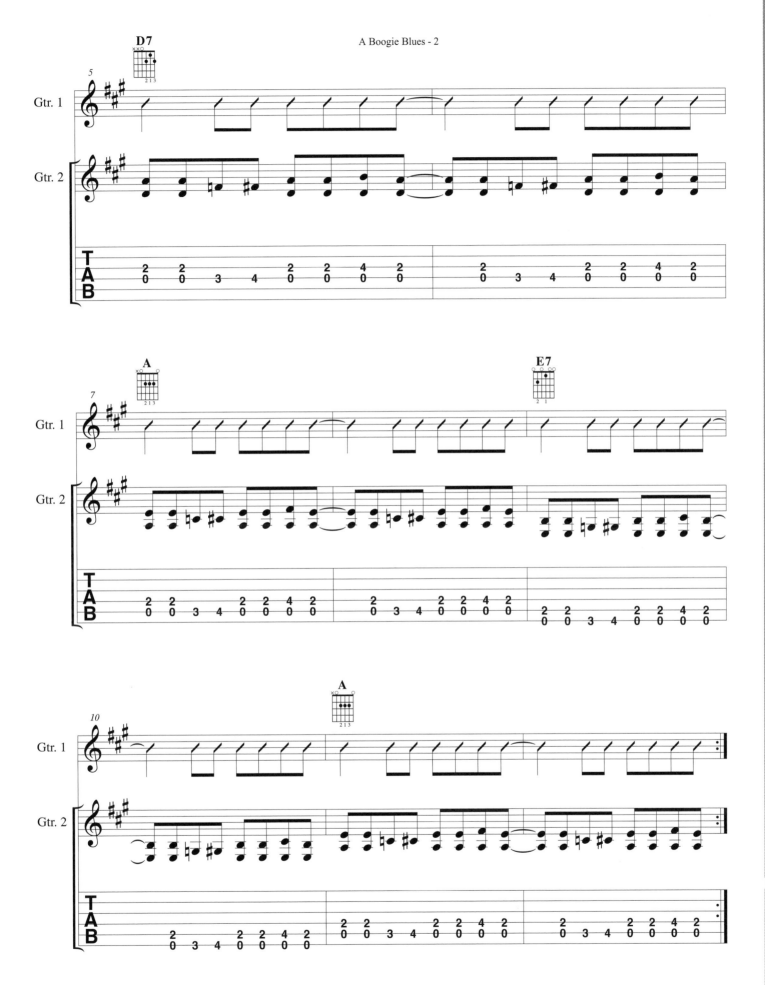

Improvising

Improvise: To create and perform music, speech, or movement on the spot.

Think of improvising as taking basic musical tools such as chords, scales, melodic riffs, and patterns and spontaneously (on the spot) reorganizing them to make something new. Throughout this book, you've been improvising accompaniments to song melodies. Every time you take the chords to a song and make up a variation on a strum or fingerpicking pattern, you are improvising.

Soloing: When a guitarist takes a solo, he or she is improvising new melodies on the spot.

Soloing is melodic improvising. When a musician takes a solo, he or she is taking the basic musical tools that are available, such as the chords, a scale that works with those chords, and a vocabulary of licks and riffs, and spontaneously reorganizing them to make new melodies. Soloing is also an opportunity for experienced performers to showcase their skills.

Improvised soloing is common in many types of music, including bluegrass, blues, and rock, and it is central to virtually every jazz performance. Even in classical music, great artists would often perform improvised cadenzas during which they could show off their virtuoso skills.

Minor Pentatonic Scale

One of the most common tools for improvising solos in blues, rock, and jazz is the five-note minor scale called the minor pentatonic. The minor pentatonic consists of the root, ♭3, 4th, 5th, and ♭7th degrees of the major scale.

A Major Scale:	A	B	C♯	D	E	F♯	G♯	A
	1	2	3	4	5	6	7	8

A Minor Pentatonic Scale:	A		C	D	E		G	A
	1		♭3	4	5		♭7	8

Note: The ♭3 and ♭7 tell you to lower the 3rd and 7th degrees by one half step. So, C♯ becomes C (not C♭) and G♯ becomes G (not G♭).

Below is the most common fingering pattern for the A minor pentatonic scale. It is presented here at the 5th fret. Practice this scale until the fingering is completely memorized and you can play it with ease.

The square indicates the root (A).

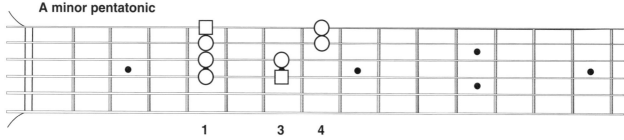

A Minor Pentatonic

Blue Notes: On page 48 you read about blue notes. Blue notes are dissonant notes that bring a gritty, blues-like feel to the music. The blue notes are the ♭3, ♭5, and ♭7. You can see that the minor pentatonic scale contains two of those blues notes.

Improvising a Blues Solo

CD Tracks 40 and 41 demonstrate improvised solos over the previous "A Boogie Blues" progression. Note the following:

- Does the soloist constantly play new things, or does he find a melody and then develop it?

- Identify new techniques that he uses such as vibrato, slurs, and string bending. (See below for more on these three techniques.)

- Imitate, or actually figure out, some of the licks he plays.

- After listening to Tracks 40 and 41, try improvising your own solos by playing along with Tracks 42 and 43.

New Phrasing Techniques

Vibrato: Vibrato adds depth and emotional impact to sustained notes. Hold the sustained note and shake your finger from side to side. It is a subtle but important effect.

Slurs: A slur is when we play the first note with our pick but then sound the next note with the left hand alone. Slurs are indicated by a curved line, connecting the two notes.

Example 1: An ascending slur is a **hammer-on:** Play the first note and then sound the second note by "hammering" your third finger down onto the string. You don't have to use a lot of force to sound the second note.

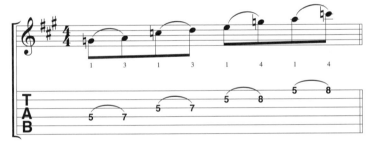

Example 2: A descending slur is a **pull-off:** Play the first note with your pick, and then pull your fourth finger off the string with just enough force to sound the note below it (your first finger must already be in place).

Example 3: String bending—As shown below, play the D at the 7th fret of the 3rd string. Using your third finger—supported by your second and first fingers—bend the string up (toward the ceiling) a whole step to E. Try this same technique on the 2nd string, bending the G up a whole step to A.

Improvising Tips

- Always know where you are in the chord progression—as you improvise, always listen to the chords and know over which chord you are improvising.

- Once you find an idea you like, repeat it; try it over each chord in the progression.

- When you discover an idea that sounds good, memorize it and use it again. It then becomes one of your improvising tools.

Roots Music

Roots music is the uniquely American melting pot of ethnic and regional folk music that eventually coalesced into modern popular music such as rock, jazz, and country. Two of the main "branches" of American roots music are "old time" mountain music and blues.

NEW CONTENT

Theory
    Key of E
    Major Scale Construction (Review)
    Ear Training

Melodic
    Key of E: **I, IV,** and **V7**
      (E, A, and B7) Chords
    Fingerpicking Pattern 6
    Chord Construction Worksheet
    Scale Construction Worksheet

Stylistic
    Roots Music
    Song: "Man of Constant Sorrow"
    Fingerstyle Blues Examples
    "Fingerstyle Blues"

Blues Soloing
    E Minor Pentatonic
    Blues Licks 1–5
    Roots Jam: "Man of Constant
      Sorrow"

Final Guitar Ensemble: "Peter Gunn"

VOCABULARY REVIEW

half step

whole step

major scale

major 3rd

minor 3rd

minor pentatonic scale

Major Scale Construction Review

Half Step: A half step (1/2) is the distance from a note to the next closest note.

Whole Step: A whole step (1) is equal to two half steps.

Major scales are constructed from the following pattern of whole steps and half steps:

Major scale:　　1　　1　　1/2　　1　　1　　1　　1/2

Remember: All adjacent natural (not sharp or flat) notes are a whole step apart (1) except E–F and B–C, which are both natural half steps (1/2).

Below are the notes from E to E. Fill in the required pattern of whole and half steps below the notes and then fill in the appropriate sharp signs for the E major scale.

E　　F　　G　　A　　B　　C　　D　　E

___　___　___　___　___　___　___

Below is a blank fretboard diagram. Draw an E major scale from open E on just the 6th string. After you draw the scale, play it with one finger. Now draw and play the E major scale on the 4th string and the 1st string. The E starting note is indicated on each string.

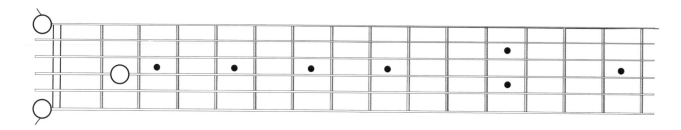

Ear Training

Sing and play the E major scale (sing in the octave most comfortable for you).

Notice the key signature: Four sharps (F♯, C♯, G♯, and D♯) is E major.

E Major Scale CD 2:46

The following fingering for the E major scale begins in 1st position and then moves up to the 2nd position (first finger at the 2nd fret) on the 2nd string. Practice this fingering for the E major scale until you can play it comfortably from memory.

Notice that in this fingering:

Instead of playing B on the open 2nd string, you play it at the 4th fret on the 3rd string, and instead of playing E on the open 1st string, you play it at the 5th fret on the 2nd string.

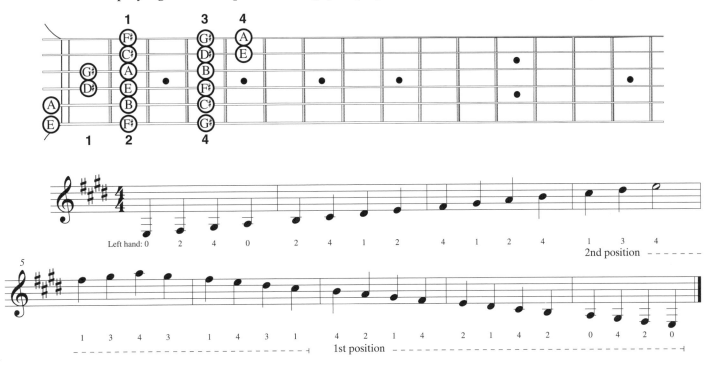

Now try "E Major Etude" based on the E major scale fingering.

E Major Etude CD 2:47

Key of E: I, IV, and V7 CD 2:48

Following is an E major scale. As you can see, in the key of E, E is the **I** chord, A is the **IV** chord, and B7 is the **V7** chord.

E	F♯	G♯	A	B	C♯	D♯	E
I	II	III	**IV**	V	VI	VII	VIII

In previous sections, you learned the E, A, and B7 chords. Here they are again for your review:

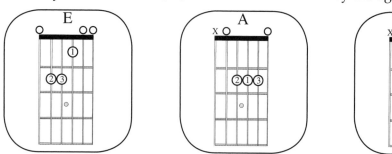

Fingerpicking Pattern 6 combines the alternating bass with fingerpicking:

- Hold the full chord.
- Your thumb plays the root (name) of the chord on beat 1.
- Your fingers (i and m) play the next three notes, on beats "+ 2 +."
- Your thumb plays the 5th of the chord (the alternate bass note) on beat 3.
- Your fingers (i and m) play the next three notes, on beats "+ 4 +."

Example 1: Fingerpicking Pattern 6 CD 2:49

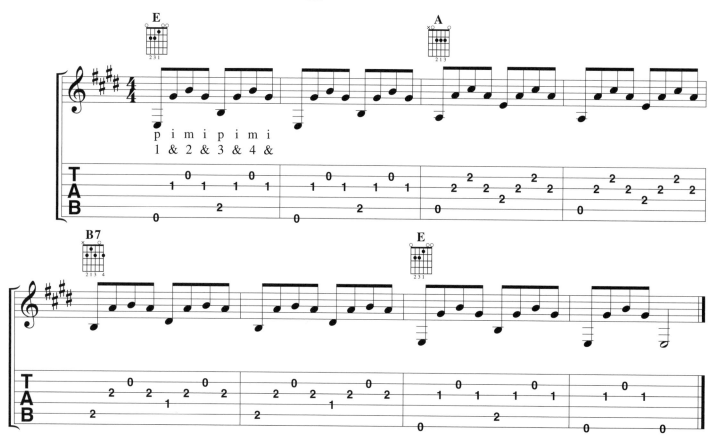

Chord Construction Review

Major 3rd = 2 whole steps

Minor 3rd = 1 $^1/_2$ whole steps

Major chords: major 3rd + minor 3rd

Minor chords: minor 3rd + major 3rd

Dominant 7th chords: major 3rd + minor 3rd + minor 3rd

Chord Construction Worksheet

Fill in the required sharp signs to match the major scale pattern of whole steps and half steps.

E   F   G   A   B   C   D   E

___   ___   ___   ___   ___   ___   ___

E Major:

What are the notes in the **I** chord?   _____   Major or minor? _____

What are the notes in the **II** chord?   _____   Major or minor?_____

What are the notes in the **III** chord?   _____   Major or minor? _____

What are the notes in the **IV** chord?   _____   Major or minor? _____

What are the notes in the **V** chord?   _____   Major or minor? _____

What are the notes in the **V7** chord?   _____   Major, minor, or dominant 7? _____

What are the notes in the **VI** chord?   _____   Major or minor? _____

Scale Construction Worksheet

The first note indicated is the root of a major scale. Fill in the rest of the notes.

Sharp keys:

G   ___   ___   ___   ___   ___   ___   ___

D   ___   ___   ___   ___   ___   ___   ___

A   ___   ___   ___   ___   ___   ___   ___

E   ___   ___   ___   ___   ___   ___   ___

B   ___   ___   ___   ___   ___   ___   ___

F♯   ___   ___   ___   ___   ___   ___   ___

Flat keys:

F   ___   ___   ___   ___   ___   ___   ___

B♭   ___   ___   ___   ___   ___   ___   ___

E♭   ___   ___   ___   ___   ___   ___   ___

A♭   ___   ___   ___   ___   ___   ___   ___

D♭   ___   ___   ___   ___   ___   ___   ___

G♭   ___   ___   ___   ___   ___   ___   ___

About Roots Music CD 2:50

Roots music is a term that refers to the uniquely American melting pot of various types of ethnic and regional folk music that eventually coalesced into modern popular music such as rock, jazz, and country. Two of the main branches of American roots music are old-time mountain music and blues.

"Old-time" refers to the early turn-of-the-century music that developed in the Appalachian Mountain area. This music was played mostly for square dances. The most common instruments were fiddle, banjo, mandolin and guitar. The songs were a mixture of compositions by American folk composers such as Stephen Foster and fiddle melodies imported from the British Isles. The songs tended to have simple pentatonic melodies (five-note scale) in major and minor keys, with simple chord progressions. The melodies were often beautiful, by virtue of their simplicity. The songs tended to fall into a few categories, love ballads, lively dances (jigs and reels), and religious songs.

We've already discussed the blues, the other main branch of American roots music. As old-time was being performed in Appalachia, blues was developing throughout the rural South. The blues sound was very different from old-time. The blues shuffle rhythm was rare in old-time music, and the dissonant blue notes that give the blues much of its personality were seldom found in the music of Appalachia.

"Man of Constant Sorrow"

"Man of Constant Sorrow" is a great example of traditional American roots music. This song was an important part of the soundtrack to the movie *O Brother, Where Art Thou?* In fact, the soundtrack to *O Brother Where Art Thou?* is a terrific example of roots music. If you can, listen to the two versions of this song on that soundtrack. The version by the Soggy Bottom Boys is fast and bluesy; the other version by folk legend John Hartford is slower with a more traditional old-time feel. Another excellent version is by the Grateful Dead's Jerry Garcia with David Grisman.

This song uses a driving strumming rhythm to propel it forward. Apply this strum pattern throughout the song. Once you can play this strum pattern at a fast tempo without faltering, begin to add some variations to the pattern.

Basic Strum Pattern CD 2:51

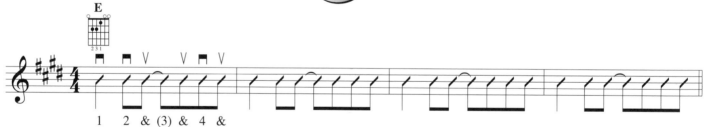

"Man of Constant Sorrow" is in the key of E, but notice how the melody has a bluesy sound. Most of the melody uses the blue notes, the ♭3rd (G) and the ♭7th (D) rather than the major 3rd (G♯) and natural 7th (D♯). In fact, the melody is based mainly on the E minor pentatonic scale. Learn both the melody and the strumming accompaniment part.

Man of Constant Sorrow

CD 2:52

Traditional

1. I_____ am a man_____ of con - stant
2. For_____ six long years_____ I've been in

sor - row.___
trou - ble,___

I've seen___ trou - ble all my
plea - sure___ here_____ on earth I

days.
found.

I_____ bid fare - well___
For_____ in this world___

to old Ken - tuck - y_____
I'm bound to ram - ble.___

the place___ where
I have___ no

I_____
friends_____

was born and raised.
to help me now.

The place where
He has no

he_____
friends_____

was born and raised.
to help him now.

1.   2.

Fingerstyle Blues

Patterns:
 CD 2:53

Most early blues songs were performed fingerstyle on acoustic guitars. Artists such as Robert Johnson and Reverend Gary Davis elevated this style of guitar playing to amazing technical heights that are still emulated by modern blues artists such as Eric Clapton and Keb Mo.

Here is a classic key-of-E blues fingerpicking pattern. Instead of strumming or fingerpicking one chord, this pattern uses three simple two-note chord fingerings to create a melodic rhythm riff. Also, this song uses a blues shuffle rhythm.

To play the E chord pattern use your right-hand "i" and "a" fingers to pluck the two-note chords and your right-hand thumb to play the low open E string:

E Chord Pattern

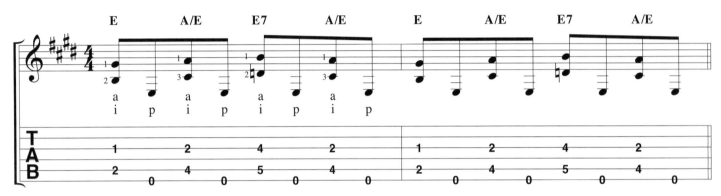

To play the A chord pattern use your right-hand "i" and "a" fingers to pluck the two-note chords and your right-hand thumb to play the low open A string. Note that the first chord requires you to barre across three strings with the first finger of your left hand:

A Chord Pattern

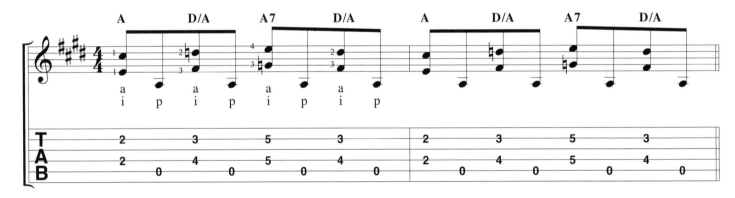

To play the B7 and A7 in measures 9 and 10, just hold these basic chord shapes and play strings 5, 4, 3, and 2.

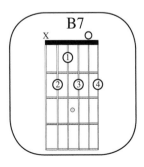

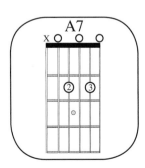

Fingerstyle Blues CD 2:54

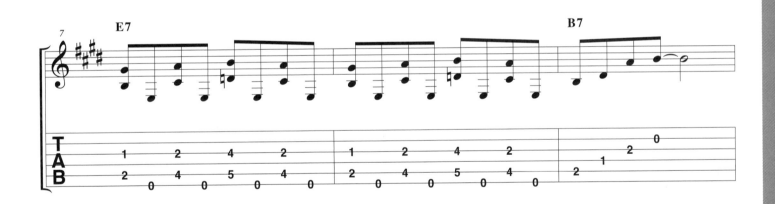

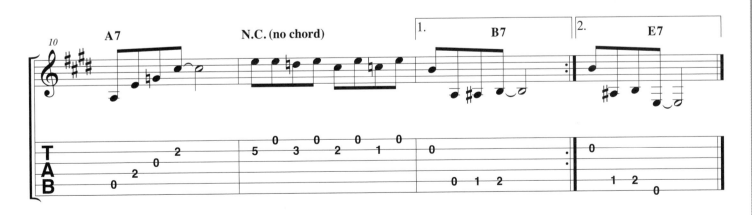

Previously you studied blues soloing using the A minor pentatonic scale (review pages 94–95). Here you will learn two patterns for the E minor pentatonic scale and use them to improvise blues solos over "Man of Constant Sorrow" and "Fingerstyle Blues."

Review: The minor pentatonic consists of the root, ♭3, 4th, 5th, and ♭7th degrees of the major scale:

E Major Scale:	E	F♯	G♯	A	B	C♯	D♯	E
	1	2	3	4	5	6	7	8
E Minor Pentatonic Scale:	E		G	A	B		D	E
	1		♭3	4	5		♭7	8

Below are two common patterns for the E minor pentatonic scale. Pattern 1 is the same one you used for A minor; here it is moved to the 1st position, making it an E minor pentatonic scale. Pattern 2 is an extension of Pattern 1. It gives you more interesting options to play. Play these patterns until you can perform them easily from memory. The square indicates the root (E).

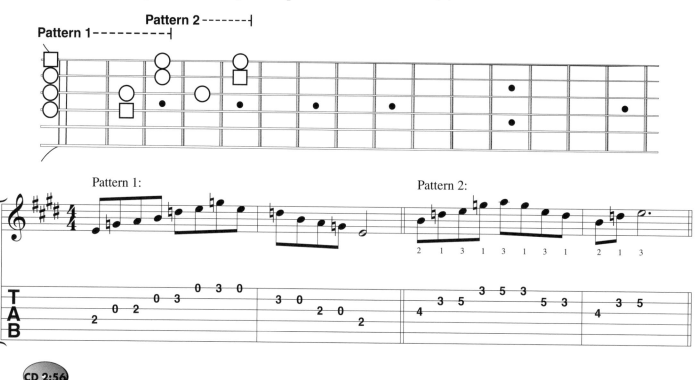

Blues Licks: A lick is a pre-determined pattern that you can plug in to your solo at will. Many licks are showy and give you a chance to show off a bit.

Lick 1: After you play the A on beat 2, slide your second finger up to the 3rd string B. Do not strike the B with your pick, just let the force of the slide sound the note (slides are a third type of slur).

Lick 2: is similar to Lick 1, only the slide is from the 2nd string D up to the 2nd string E.

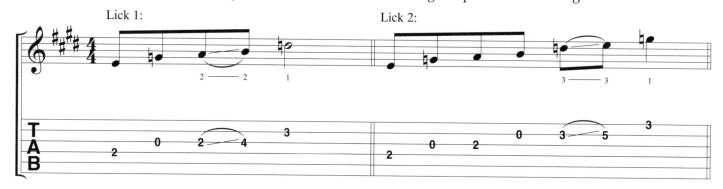

SECTION 9 • Blues Soloing in E

Lick 3: This one is a common blues lick. Play the 3rd string A and then immediately slide up to B. Slide into each B the same way. Listen to the recording to get a feel for it.

Licks 4 and 5: These licks combine a hammer-on and a pull-off into one smooth three-note slur. In Lick 4, hammer from open E to G and then pull-off from G to E. In lick 5, hammer from G to A and then pull-off back to G.

Lick 4:   Lick 5:

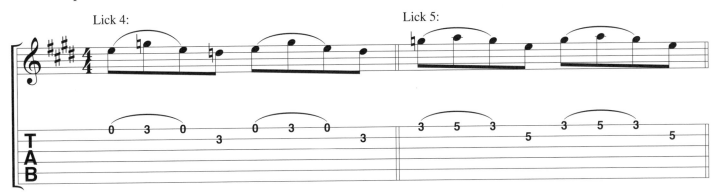

Roots Jam: Apply these licks and patterns to playing a solo and fills (licks played behind and between the vocal phrases) on "Man of Constant Sorrow." Listen to the fills and solo played by the guitarist on CD 2, Track 57. CD 2 Track 58 is the same song but with no guitar. Improvise your own fills and solo.

Man of Constant Sorrow

Demo: CD 2:57   Play-Along: CD 2:58

Traditional

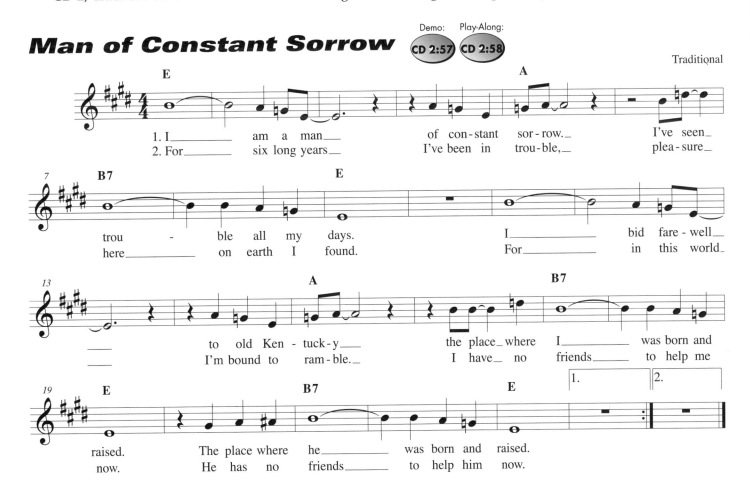

In 1958 "Peter Gunn," a stylish, gritty, black-and-white private-eye drama debuted on NBC. Starring Craig Stevens as the dapper and sophisticated private eye, the series was set to an infectious jazz-driven soundtrack written by Henry Mancini, one of the greatest and most successful Hollywood film score writers ever. Mancini's film and TV scores, blending cool West Coast jazz, hip driving bass lines, and lots of slick blues inflections, established the standard for all film and television detective and spy genre soundtracks soon to come in the '60s, including "The James Bond Theme" and "Secret Agent Man." Listen to the original Mancini soundtrack recording or to Duane Eddy's 1960 hit. There is also a good version by the Art of Noise, featuring Duane Eddy on guitar.

Performance Notes

This song is in the key of E—four sharps. But, because of its blues flavor, most of the Gs and Ds are natural (review blue notes on page 48). This ensemble arrangement of "Peter Gunn" brings together everything you've learned throughout this book. Try to learn all three guitar parts.

Guitar 1:

- This is a divisi part, meaning: If more than one person is assigned to Guitar 1, some can play the top part (stems up), which is the melody, and some can play the harmony part (stems down). If only one person is assigned to this part, he or she should play the melody (stems up).
- This part enters on the fourth bar of the intro with a doubling of the bass line, one octave higher.
- Measure 8 of the melody part contains a high B—7th fret, 1st string—and an F on the 6th fret, 2nd string.
- The B section is basically a short instrumental solo.
- The C section contains a hand-clap section. You have to be quick to go from the last measure of clapping directly back into your guitar part.
- Notice the accent marks four bars from the end. Accent the note and then cut it short. Cut it short by releasing your left hand pressure after each note.
- In the last measure, the dash above the first E tells you to play that note long, and the dot above the second E tells you to cut that note short.

Guitar 2:

- This part enters on the third bar of the Intro with a harmony to the bass line.
- Make sure to use a palm mute to play this part. Lay the palm of your pick hand gently on the strings just in front of the bridge. This technique will produce a short, muffled, percussive attack.
- In section A, Guitar 2 switches to a ska or reggae-style rhythm guitar part. Play the E7 chord as indicated. The rhythm is: 1 2+ 3 4 1 2+ 3 4. You should strike the chord only on 2, the "and" of 2, and on beat 4.
- The dash above the first E7 rhythm slash tells you to play that chord long (for its full value); the dot above the next rhythm slash tells you to cut that chord short.
- In Section B the rhythm guitar fills in with a few important accented chords that fall in the cracks in a call-and-response pattern with the melody.
- Section C contains a hand-clap section. You have to be quick to go from the last measure of clapping directly back into your guitar part.
- Notice the accent marks four bars from the end. Accent the note and then cut it short. Cut it short by releasing your left-hand pressure after each note.

Guitar 3:

- This guitar enters with the signature "Peter Gunn" bass-line riff. Guitar 3 is the bass part. If you are doubling the part with a bass guitar, use a very treble, twangy sound. Use your lead pickup if you are playing electric guitar, and add some reverb and a palm mute.
- In Section B this part fills in with a few important accented bass notes that fall in the cracks in a call-and-response pattern with the melody.
- Notice the accent marks four bars from the end. Accent the note and then cut it short. Cut it short by releasing your left hand pressure after each note.
- In the last measure, the dash above the first E tells you to play that note long, and the dot above the second E tells you to cut that note short.

Peter Gunn
(Guitar 1)

Complete Version: CD 2:59 Play-Along Version: CD 2:60

HENRY MANCINI
Arr. by Rob Goldsmith

Peter Gunn
(Guitar 2)

HENRY MANCINI

Palm mute

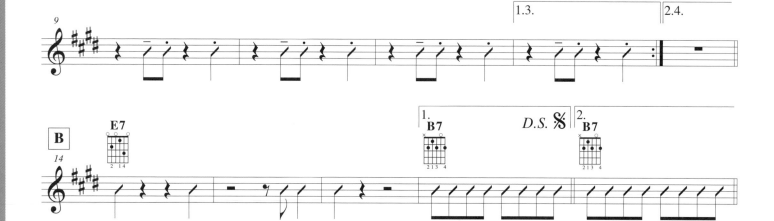

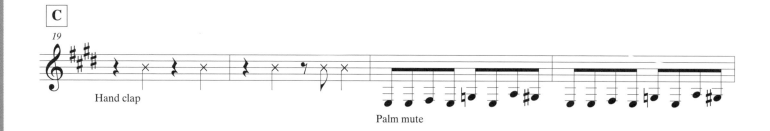

Hand clap

Palm mute

Peter Gunn
(Guitar 3)

HENRY MANCINI

Palm mute throughout

About the Authors

Aaron Stang is the author of Alfred Publishing's *21st Century Guitar Method*—one of the most popular guitar methods in publication—which has been translated into Spanish, French, German, and Japanese. Aaron is a featured artist on the Grammy™ award-winning CD, *Henry Mancini, Pink Guitar* (Solid Air Records). *Pink Guitar* won the Grammy™ for Best Pop Instrumental Album at the 47th Annual Grammy™ Awards. Aaron is a managing editor for Alfred Publishing where he has overseen the publication of hundreds of books and videos. Aaron performs in concerts and folk festivals throughout South Florida.

Bill Purse is Chair of the guitar and music technology departments at Duquesne University (Pittsburgh, PA), and he is past chair of the MENC/GAMA/NAMM Guitar Task Force—helping to create over 1000 new class-guitar programs nationally. Purse received Duquesne University's 1996 Presidents award for excellence in scholarship and a 2001 Lifetime Achievement Award for guitar pedagogy and performance. Bill has toured worldwide with the synthesizer ensemble, Aergo, and is the producer, arranger, and guitarist/musical director for the Duquesne faculty guitar ensemble, Catch 22. Bill has written and arranged numerous published words including "Europa" and "Classical Gas" for the *21st Century Guitar Ensemble* series and *Home Recording Basics* for Warner Bros. Publications.